3
Day
Loan

Climate Alarmism Reconsidered

Climate Alarmism Reconsidered

ROBERT L. BRADLEY JR

The Institute of Economic Affairs

First published in Great Britain in 2003 by
The Institute of Economic Affairs
2 Lord North Street
Westminster
London SW1P 3LB
in association with Profile Books Ltd

A CIP catalogue record for this book is available from the British Library.

ISBN 0 255 36541 1

Many IEA publications are translated into languages other than English or
are reprinted. Permission to translate or to reprint should be sought from the
Director General at the address above.

Typeset in Stone by MacGuru Ltd
info@macguru.org.uk

Printed and bound in Great Britain by Hobbs the Printers

CONTENTS

THE AUTHOR

Robert L. Bradley Jr is president of the Institute for Energy Research in Houston, Texas, and a senior research fellow at the University of Houston. He is author of *The Mirage of Oil Protection* (1989), *Oil, Gas, and Government: The US Experience* (2 vols, 1996) and *Julian Simon and the Triumph of Energy Sustainability* (2000), as well as shorter studies on energy history and policy. He received the Julian L. Simon Memorial Award for 2002 for his work on energy sustainability issues. Bradley received his BA in economics from Rollins College, where he received the S. Truman Olin Award in Economics. He received an MA in economics from the University of Houston and a PhD with distinction in political economy from International College.

FOREWORD

It has become accepted wisdom that human activity is changing the climate for the worse, and policy activism is necessary to transform the energy mix away from carbon-based fuels. This view is propagated through the media and at educational institutions throughout the UK and the EU more generally. Unfortunately, it is rarely exposed to critical appraisal, turning what should be a live intellectual debate into 'indoctrination' rather than 'education'.

Hobart Paper 146 by Rob Bradley of the Institute for Energy Research in Houston, Texas, is a welcome reassessment of much of the accepted wisdom regarding climate change. His wide-ranging analysis documents a number of weaknesses in the argument that we are facing serious adverse impacts from climate change. His argument gains weight when the general context of energy sustainability debate is considered, where the 'alarmists' on fossil-fuel reliance have been wrong time and again.

There is no longer an energy depletion problem: the evidence is clear that, as long as governments do not interfere, new sources of energy can be found to meet demand at constant costs or better – not just for the next generation or two but for centuries ahead. Pollution is declining dramatically in the USA and in the EU. Energy is used with greater and greater efficiency, as the energy required per unit of output decreases. And market forces have effectively addressed energy reliability/security challenges as compared with government activism. This is not to say that energy problems will not arise, but unhampered market processes inspire solutions to real problems.

There is much concern about anthropogenic (man-made) climate change or global warming. But scary climate scenarios are not supported by the *balance of evidence*. What is known with far more confidence is that a moderately warmer and wetter world has significant benefits to offset costs for many decades to come.

It might be argued that we should take a 'precautionary approach'. Even if serious adverse effects from anthropogenic warming are highly unlikely, it is often suggested that we should take action to avoid any possible problems. Such an approach, argues Bradley, would be seriously mistaken. Policy activism that makes energy less available and affordable has an opportunity cost, which includes the cost of forgone wealth and forgone environmental benefits from imposing inefficient policies on the economy.

Climate alarmists and policy activists have pointed to market failure as a justification for policy activism, as if a perfect government can automatically correct an imperfect market. When the concept of government failure is also taken into account, the case for policy activism begins to look unattractive. Activist policies are sure to lead to the creation of rent-seeking groups who will drive policy not towards theoretical perfection but towards maximisation of the welfare of rent-seekers.

Bradley's approach recommends policy activism of a different sort from that normally prescribed in the climate debate. Governments can and should follow a number of 'no regrets' policies that reduce emissions but do not create losers such as consumers or taxpayers. Free-market activism includes not just voluntarism, but the removal of implicit and explicit government subsidies for carbon fuels and for products and services that use carbon fuels intensively.

Bradley argues, more generally, that the major threat to energy sustainability is *statism*, whereby government energy planning creates the problems that non-politicised market processes work to prevent. In the developing world in particular, governments should not impoverish their citizens by denying them secure, transferable property rights, voluntary exchange and earnings retention. In this way the 1.6 billion energy poor can access electricity and protect themselves from life's many uncertainties, only one of which is climate change.

Bradley's multi-disciplinary study deserves careful attention from policy-makers, opinion-formers and educators. If Europe does not wake up to what is a two-sided intellectual debate, the rest of the world will move forward without us.

The views expressed in this Hobart Paper are, as in all IEA publications, those of the author and not those of the Institute (which has no corporate view), its managing trustees, Academic Advisory Council members or senior staff.

PHILIP BOOTH

Editorial and Programme Director,
Institute of Economic Affairs
Professor of Insurance and Risk Management,
Sir John Cass Business School, City
University
July 2003

ACKNOWLEDGEMENTS

This monograph, the culmination of several years of interest and research on different questions of climate and related energy policy, has been greatly improved by the comments and suggestions of many individuals. The author wishes to thank, without implication, J. Allen Carruth (Kirby Hall School), Richard Fulmer (Institute for Energy Research), Marlo Lewis (Competitive Enterprise Institute), Richard Lindzen (Massachusetts Institute of Technology), Brian Mannix (Mercatus Center, George Mason University), Patrick Michaels (University of Virginia), Julian Morris (International Policy Network), Colin Robinson (University of Surrey), and two anonymous referees for helpful comments.

SUMMARY

- The energy sustainability issues of resource depletion, reliability (security) and pollution have been effectively addressed by market entrepreneurship, technology and, in the absence of private property rights, measured regulation. Continuing improvement is expected.
- The remaining carbon energy-related sustainability issue concerns anthropogenic (man-made) climate change. Current levels of atmospheric greenhouse gas (GHG) concentrations are approximately 52 per cent above pre-industrial levels with an associated increase in global warming potential of 66 per cent. Emissions released in the mining, transportation and combustion of oil, natural gas and coal account for most of this accumulation.
- The balance of evidence points towards a benign temperature 'greenhouse signal'. A greenhouse signal has not been identified with weather extremes or 'surprises'.
- Enhanced atmospheric carbon dioxide (CO_2) concentrations create tangible benefits to offset any costs associated with anthropogenic climate change.
- Liberal energy markets foster wealth creation, adaptation and social resilience – a positive strategy to deal with inevitable climate change, natural and anthropogenic. In addition, free-market reforms in the energy sector harness self-interest

in energy efficiency, which has historically tended to reduce GHG emissions per unit of energy.

- Mandatory GHG emission reductions beyond 'no regrets' actions produce costs in excess of benefits under realistic assumptions, including discounting future benefits (if discernible) to compare with near-term costs.
- Serious efforts to equilibrate the carbon cycle will have to employ novel sequestration strategies given increasing energy usage, supply constraints with renewable energies and political and economic limitations with nuclear power.
- Activist proposals for GHG reductions such as cap-and-trade programmes should be cognisant of the unintended consequences of open-ended regulatory regimes driven by temporary political majorities.
- The *precautionary principle* should be applied to government intervention limiting GHG emissions (e.g. the Kyoto Protocol), not just to acts of man on the natural environment. The economic risks of intervention, in other words, must be evaluated along with environmental ones.
- The major threat to energy sustainability is *statism*, not depletion, pollution, reliability or anthropogenic climate change. Major government interventions in energy markets, such as price controls, access restrictions or carbon suppression, create the energy problems that non-politicised, free-market processes work to prevent.

FIGURES

Climate Alarmism Reconsidered

Climate Alarmism Reconsidered

1 INTRODUCTION

The interaction between man and climate has interested scientists and the public for centuries. Global warming and cooling scares pre-date the current concern over global warming that began in the 1980s.[1] Most recently, new theories and improved detection techniques have raised concern that man's influence is altering global climate beyond its natural fluctuation through an *enhanced greenhouse effect*.[2] In the context of energy sustainability issues, anthropogenic (man-made) climate change has become the major issue confronting the modern carbon energy economy. Other energy 'sustainability' issues such as depletion, pollution and reliability (security) have proven amenable to market incentives, technological progress and, in some cases, government regulation.[3] The prophets of carbon energy alarmism have been proven wrong time and again along the way.

1 James Fleming, *Historical Perspectives on Climate Change*, Oxford University Press, Oxford, 1998, pp. 129–37.

2 For an explanation of the enhanced greenhouse effect within a case for global warming concern, see Tom Wigley, 'The Science of Climate Change', in Eileen Claussen (ed.), *Climate Change: Science, Strategies, & Solutions*, Brill, for the Pew Center on Global Climate Change, Boston, MA, 2001, pp. 7–24.

3 This essay will not address the debate between market-failure proponents of environmental regulation and libertarian proponents of free-market environmentalism who believe in property-rights reforms to attempt to internalise environmental externalities. Relatively successful regulation, in any case, has addressed well-defined problems and been undertaken at a pace in congruence with technological change and public understanding and support.

Figure 1   **Economic-energy-climate-policy nexus**

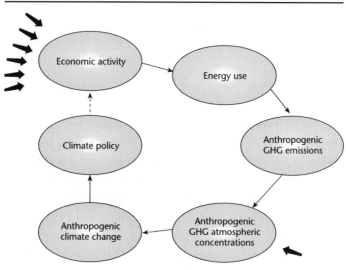

This monograph addresses several key questions. What does atmospheric science (climatology) currently conclude about the anthropogenic influence on global and regional climate? What does the relatively new speciality of *climate economics*, or more broadly *climate political economy*, conclude about the future benefits and costs of the human influence on climate? And most importantly, what public policies towards greenhouse gas emissions are supported by *the balance of evidence presented by climate science and climate economics*? These questions involve six linkages shown in Figure 1 which range from economic activity all the way to the manner in which climate policy impacts on economic activity.

Answers to these questions point towards *climate optimism* and *policy restraint*. The human influence on climate, tending towards warmth, moisture and carbon fertilisation, promises significant benefits to offset anticipated costs. The evidence to date of the anthropogenic influence has been *moderate* and *benign*. Climate models suggesting a far worse future have trouble squaring this with the past and depend on highly simplified physical representations of climate. Such simplification is prone to being falsified by more realistic (and complicated) climate processes that are now becoming better understood.

Turning to public policy, government intervention to 'protect the climate' or 'slow climate change' has a surprisingly limited impact on overall carbon emissions and a predictably large negative impact on energy availability, dependability and affordability. The panacea of renewable energy is problematic on environmental and non-environmental grounds upon close inspection. Reduced overall energy usage is not an option. As history has shown, total energy consumption can rise even as energy intensity per unit of economic activity falls. A hydrogen energy economy could still be fuelled by carbon-based energy, and the commercialisation of hydrogen as a mass energy carrier remains decades away, as it has been for well over a century.

Increasing energy sustainability points towards an *enhanced carbon energy era* where ever more innovations with crude oil, natural gas and coal – and a growing number of close substitutes in between – make energy more plentiful and cleaner for an open-ended future.

The critics of carbon energies have not proved that there is a problem that justifies a radical departure from a consumer-oriented energy economy. Nor do they propose adequate solutions to the problems they suppose exist. Human ingenuity within a framework of private property, free markets and problem-based regulatory reform has made carbon energies one of the most significant economic and environmental triumphs of our time. The true threat to energy sustainability is the activist/alarmist policies that are being advanced in the name of energy sustainability – a conundrum that the best evidence and arguments of both natural and social science warn against.

2 CARBON ENERGY SUSTAINABILITY

There is a strong positive correlation between rising living standards and societal reliance on private property rights, market processes and the rule of law.[1] The *carbon energy* economy has been part of this success. Energy has grown less polluting and more abundant, affordable and reliable throughout history, and particularly in the second half of the last century, especially in market settings. The empirical record contradicts the *energy Malthusians* who have long predicted increasing scarcity, physical shortages, worsening pollution and general crises from increasing dependence upon carbon energies.

Growing supply

Global discoveries of crude oil, natural gas and coal have outpaced consumption since their commercialisation in the nineteenth

---

1   For documentation on numerous trends in human progress, see Theodore Caplow et al., *The First Measured Century*, AEI Press, Washington, DC, 2001; Stephen Moore and Julian Simon, *It's Getting Better All the Time: 100 Greatest Trends of the Last 100 Years*, Cato Institute, Washington, DC, 2000; and Björn Lomborg, *The Skeptical Environmentalist: Measuring the True State of the World*, Cambridge University Press, Cambridge, 2001. For an overview of the growing role of free-market policies in the twentieth century, see Daniel Yergin and Joseph Stanislaw, *The Commanding Heights: The Battle between Government and the Marketplace That Is Remaking the Modern World*, Simon & Schuster, New York, 1998.

Figure 2   **Carbon energy usage and potential supply**
Quadrillion Btus

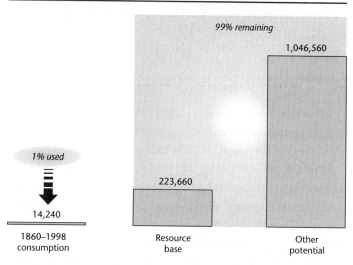

Source: Intergovernmental Panel on Climate Change, *Climate Change 2001: Mitigation*, Cambridge University Press, Cambridge, 2001, p. 236

century. Future supplies are considered abundant for at least the twenty-first century. A study by the Intergovernmental Panel on Climate Change (IPCC), a study group established in 1988 by the United Nations and other world organisations to study the climate issue, estimates that total consumption of carbon energies in the period 1860–1998 totals just 1.1 per cent of what physically remains in the ground pending future production and consumption, as illustrated in Figure 2.[2]

2   IPCC, *Climate Change 2001: Mitigation*, Cambridge University Press, Cambridge, 2001, p. 236. Carbon energies refers to conventional and un-conventional oil, conventional and unconventional natural gas (including

Of the total remaining supply, less than one fifth is either located and ready-to-be-produced reserves or reserves awaiting commercialisation given likely prices and technology. The greatest proportion is 'additional occurrences', conventional and unconventional, that would require higher prices and/or further improvements in technology to be economically recoverable. But the very long-time horizon involved in their utilisation suggests that a gradual commercialisation of the 'non-commercial' is quite possible.

Statistics confirm that global carbon energies are an expanding resource, not a depleting one as suggested in the textbook treatment of a 'finite' resource. The world's proved reserves of crude oil are over twenty times greater today than they were when such record-keeping began over half a century ago. World natural gas reserves are five times greater than they were in the mid-1960s. Coal reserves are four times greater than originally estimated half a century ago and twice as great as all the known oil and gas reserves combined on an energy-equivalent basis.[3]

How can 'depletable' carbon energies expand faster than consumption decade after decade? An unconventional explanation is that carbon energies are not (or not only) geologically transformed plant and animal debris (fossil fuels) but a primordial part of a

---

deep-ocean clathrates) and coal. Reserves are found ('proved') supply; resources are potential reserves assuming anticipated changes in technology and price; 'additional occurrences' are estimated physical supply beyond the supply that is expected to turn into resources (later reserves).

3   These statistics come from Robert Bradley and Richard Fulmer, *Energy: The Master Resource*, Institute for Energy Research, Houston, TX, forthcoming. Earlier estimates are provided in Robert Bradley, *Julian Simon and the Triumph of Energy Sustainability*, American Legislative Exchange Council, Washington, DC, 2000, pp. 28–31.

deep, hot biosphere.[4] If this is true, super-abundant carbon energies are seeping up from far below to reach the drill bit. A more conventional explanation is that human ingenuity and the financial capital required to extract mineral energies are not depleting but infinitely expansible. Consequently, improving performance can win over diminishing returns.[5]

Depletionists subscribe to a *bell curve* view whereby global oil, gas or coal output increases, peaks and then declines. This model assumes a fixed supply – or really fixed technology and unchanged knowledge applied to the resource base. Yet improving knowledge and new applications of capital move any real-world bell curve upward and to the right. Whole new bell curves can be created from near-substitutes to crude oil such as heavy oil (bitumen) and orimulsion whereby the low-grade solids are upgraded on-site to refining quality.

The march of substitution from technological change theoretically ends with agricultural cultivation of usable oils (bio-fuels). Thus while *crude* oil and *natural* gas may be physically 'depletable', oil and gas can and may well morph over time into non-depletable, although always finite, supplies.[6] The expansive *resource pyramid* view of carbon energy supply is contrasted with the depletionists'

---

4 See Thomas Gold, *The Deep Hot Biosphere*, Copernicus, New York, 1999. For a review of Gold's theory that finds it plausible among controversial scientific ideas, see Robert Ehrlich, *Nine Crazy Ideas in Science*, Princeton University Press, Princeton, NJ, 2001, ch. 7.

5 Morris Adelman, 'Trends in the Price and Supply of Oil', in Julian Simon (ed.), *The State of Humanity*, Blackwell, Cambridge, MA, 1995, p. 292.

6 Commercial inter-fuel expansion also includes gas-to-liquids conversion where non-commercial or 'standard' natural gas reserves are refined into light oil products such as motor fuel. See, for example, Barbara Shook, 'Cobalt-Based Catalyst Seen Key to Shell's Growth in GTL Sector', *Natural Gas Week*, 16 October 2000, pp. 2–3.

Figure 3   **Energy future: two views**

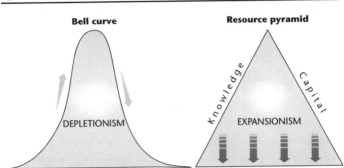

Note: *Depletionism* is based on a known fixed supply whose production increases, peaks and declines owing to diminishing returns overtaking improvements in knowledge. *Expansionism*, or increasing supply over time, is based on the open-ended nature of knowledge, increasing financial capital, expanding substitutability, and free-market incentives.

bell curve in Figure 3. The open-ended nature of supply (illustrated by the bottomless pyramid) results since knowledge and financial capital are infinitely expansive.

A global 'depletion signal' has not emerged for any major carbon energy source, although many specific fields and mines have been produced to their economic limit.[7] A broad view of 'depletion', however, could also apply to renewable energy projects that have siting constraints for economic and environmental reasons

---

7   This micro-behaviour has and still does inspire forecasts of the end of low-cost oil despite admissions by some environmentalists that depletion is no longer a primary sustainability issue. For examples of supply alarmism, see Colin Campbell, *The Coming Oil Crisis*, Multi-Science Publishing, Essex, 1997; Kenneth Deffeyes, *Hubbert's Peak*, Princeton University Press, Princeton, NJ, 2001; and James McKenzie, 'Oil as a Finite Resource: When Is Global Production Likely to Peak?', World Resources Institute, March 1996.

as discussed below.[8] Just as mines are worked in order of their most productive seams, renewable projects begin from the most favourable locations and work down to sites of lesser quality.

Declining pollution

Air, land and water pollution associated with carbon energies is declining in the UK, the USA and much of the rest of the world – even as carbon energy consumption and other 'human pressures' increase. A doubling of real gross domestic product (GDP) since 1970 and a slight increase in overall energy use of 13 per cent in the UK have been accompanied by the following reductions in air pollutants: sulphur dioxide (SO_2): 83 per cent; nitrogen oxides (NO_X): 33 per cent; particulate matter (PM_{10}): 67 per cent; carbon monoxide (CO): 58 per cent; and volatile organic compounds (VOCs): 30 per cent. Figure 4 shows the overall reduction in aggregate emissions of these air pollutants between 1970 and 2001 – 60 per cent – compared with several economic and energy growth indicators.

Large air emission reductions in the UK have largely resulted from the 1990s 'dash for gas' when natural gas from the North Sea became available, the coal industry was privatised, and new-capacity decisions were left to the market. Falling gas prices, rapid advances in gas-fired combined-cycle technologies and the environmental advantages of gas accelerated the retirement of inefficient coal plants, and gas became the fuel of choice for new capacity in the UK. Between 1990 and 2000, electricity generated from coal fell by almost one half, while gas-fired power increased from virtually nothing to 134 terawatt hours, a 39 per cent share of

8   See below, pp. 38–9, 135–9.

Figure 4 **UK growth versus aggregate air pollution emissions**
%, 1970–2001

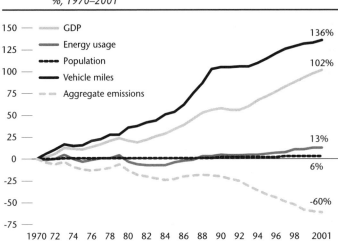

Sources: GDP and Primary Energy Consumption (temperature corrected): Department of Trade and Industry, http://www.dti.gov.uk/energy/inform/energy_indicators/ind11.pdf; population (in millions): Office of National Statistics, www.statistics.gov.uk; pollution (in million tonnes) and road traffic (in billion miles): Department of Environment, Food and Rural Affairs (DEFRA), http://www.defra.gov.uk/environment/statistics/eiyp/general/gen56.htm; pollution charts (2.18, 2.20, 2.21, and 2.24): http://www.defra.gov.uk/environment/statistics/des/airqual/allfigs.htm.

the total market. Meanwhile, remaining coal capacity was retrofitted with low NO_X burners to reduce emissions.[9]

Urban air quality in the USA has also substantially improved as economic activity has accelerated. The US Environmental Protection Agency reports that aggregate air emissions of the six principal air pollutants fell 25 per cent between 1970 and 2001. US

---

9   Department of Trade and Industry, *Energy Projections for the UK*, Energy Paper 68, 2001, pp. 33, 37, 76. With existing coal plants operating at a 36 per cent efficiency factor, gas-fired combined-cycle improved from 45 per cent to beyond 50 per cent efficiency (ibid., p. 33).

CLIMATE ALARMISM RECONSIDERED

Figure 5   **US growth versus aggregate air pollution emissions**
%, 1970–2001

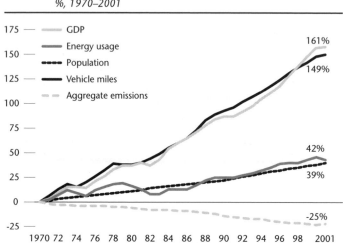

Source: US Environmental Protection Agency, *Latest Findings on National Air Quality: 2001 Status and Trends*, US EPA, Washington, DC, 2002, p. 4.

emissions of CO declined 19 per cent, VOCs fell 38 per cent, SO_2 dropped 44 per cent, PM_{10} fell 76 per cent, and lead declined 98 per cent. During the same 31 years, the US population grew by one third, GDP increased 161 per cent, energy consumption increased 42 per cent, and vehicle miles travelled increased 149 per cent, as seen in Figure 5.[10]

Nitrogen oxide (NO_x), a smog precursor, has increased 15 per cent in the USA since 1970. However, a 3 per cent decrease has been recorded since 1992.[11] Improving technology and new

---

10   US Environmental Protection Agency, *Latest Findings on National Air Quality: 2001 Status and Trends*, September 2002, p. 17.

11   Ibid., pp. 2–3.

30

regulatory requirements portend a new round of reductions in NO_x in the years ahead in urban areas not in compliance with the US Clean Air Act. In Houston, Texas, for example, plans are being implemented to reduce NO_x emissions by 75 per cent by 2007 to eliminate ozone episode days entirely. Such improvement would mirror the progress that the Los Angeles Basin has experienced in the past two decades in reducing ozone formation (smog).[12]

The emission of air toxins associated with carbon energy combustion has also shown abatement since measurements recently began. US air toxins declined over 20 per cent during the 1990s with the emission of the 33 toxins of most concern to human health dropping 31 per cent. Ambient concentrations of benzene, which is associated with gasoline emissions, dropped by 47 per cent between 1994 and 2000.[13]

Significant progress in air quality has also been measured in Canada, western European states and other wealthy countries as technology and regulatory standards have matured.[14] Over time, rising incomes in the developing world can be expected to result in cleaner environments as well.[15]

Other petroleum-related statistics from the USA suggest increasing sustainability. Oil spills in US navigable waters have fallen nearly 60 per cent during the last decade. Improvements in prevention training, faster response times, better clean-up technologies and new investments in double-hulled tankers have made damaging oil spills (such as occurred in 1989 with the *Exxon*

---

12 Bradley, *Julian Simon*, op. cit., pp. 80–81.

13 US Environmental Protection Agency, op. cit., pp. 20–21.

14 Lomborg, op. cit., ch. 15; International Energy Agency, *Toward a Sustainable Energy Future*, OECD, Paris, 2001, pp. 43–5.

15 Lomborg, op. cit., pp. 175–7.

Valdez) almost a thing of the past.[16] Similar reforms are taking place in the EU given recent spills.

Oil pipeline leakage in the USA has dropped 60 per cent since the early 1970s.[17] Methane emissions from natural gas pipelines have declined also.[18] Worker safety as measured by fatalities, injuries and 'incidents' has improved significantly.[19] In all, the world's leading consumer of carbon energies has recorded positive gains in virtually every category of energy sustainability.

Improving quality

The *quality* of energy products has dramatically improved in non-environmental areas as well.

Financial products developed in recent decades allow sophisticated energy users to lock in prices and supply over a variety of time horizons. Risk management in organised futures markets or with over-the-counter (tailor-made) products eliminates the need for government intervention to promote 'fuel diversity' since diversity is not important for its own sake but only as a strategy to mitigate supply and price volatility.[20] Price and supply certainty can also improve the risk profile of projects to facilitate financing. Liquid forward curves for fuel inputs and electricity output will be

16 American Petroleum Institute, 'Oil Spills in US Navigable Waters', 18 January 2001.

17 Association of Oil Pipe Lines, 'Safety Record', available at <www.aopl.org/safety/record.html>.

18 US Energy Information Administration, *Annual Energy Review 2000*, Department of Energy, Washington, DC, 2001, pp. 9, 323.

19 American Petroleum Institute, 'Workplace Safety for the US Petroleum Industry', 21 January 2001. Available at www.api.org at http://api-ec.api.org/filelibrary/POEOverview.pdf.

20 Bradley, *Julian Simon*, op. cit., pp. 57–60.

necessary to help attract an estimated $4.2 trillion in capital that will be needed between now and 2030 for new power generation capacity globally.[21]

The privatisation of energy assets has improved physical operation and consumer services in a number of countries.[22] However, many privatisation opportunities remain. Of the 21.2 million barrels of oil lifted per day in 2001 by the world's top five producers, 88 per cent was controlled by four state oil companies and 12 per cent by Exxon Mobil.[23] A greater role for private companies is urgently needed in Russia, for example, where gas production has been stagnant and Gazprom is the sole exporter of Russian gas to western Europe.[24] Downstream privatisation is also needed.

Increasing consumption/falling intensity

Rising energy consumption in both the developed and developing world is virtually assured. The forecast statistics presented below have profound implications for global carbon emissions and the effectiveness of the Kyoto Protocol, the subject of a later section.[25]

The forecasting arm of the US Department of Energy, the Energy Information Administration (EIA), predicts that global energy demand will increase by 58 per cent (1.9 per cent annually) between 2001 and 2025. Carbon energies are anticipated to increase their market share in the same period from 86 per cent

---

21 International Energy Agency, *World Energy Outlook 2002*, OECD, Paris, 2002, p. 26.

22 See, generally, Arthur Andersen and the *Petroleum Economist*, *The Guide to World Energy Privatisation*, Petroleum Economist Ltd, London, May 2001.

23 Energy Intelligence Group, reprinted in Alexei Barrionuevo, 'How Technicians at Oil Giant Turned Revolutionaries', *Wall Street Journal*, 10 February 2003, p. A1.

24 International Energy Agency, *World Energy Outlook 2002*, op. cit., pp. 277–80.

25 See below, pp. 100–107.

to 88 per cent. Electricity use in the forecast grows at a higher rate of 2.4 per cent annually, an overall increase of 77 per cent. This growth assumes a reduction in energy intensity per economic unit of 1.2 per cent annually.[26]

The International Energy Agency predicts a 66 per cent increase in world energy consumption up to 2030, a 1.7 per cent annual growth rate, with electricity demand increasing at a higher annual rate of 2.4 per cent. These projections include an anticipated decline in energy intensity of 1.2 per cent annually. The global market share of carbon energies in the commercial energy mix will increase from 87 per cent to 89 per cent by 2030, with over 90 per cent of the increase in total demand coming from oil, gas or coal.[27]

Energy intensity – the amount of energy used per unit of economic output – is declining in most regions of the world. In the USA, for example, a unit of economic output in 2001 required 55 per cent of the energy the same unit required in 1970.[28] New energy applications are increasing productivity and enhancing the quality of life. Population growth and new energy uses are increasing total energy consumption even as energy efficiency improves – not only in the USA but also in Europe, where annual consumption is anticipated to rise 0.8 per cent and annual energy intensity to fall by 1.2 per cent by 2030.[29]

The reality of growing energy use *and* efficiency, coupled

---

26 Energy Information Administration, *International Energy Outlook 2003*, US Department of Energy, Washington, DC, 2003, pp. 1–4, 183, 190.

27 International Energy Agency, *World Energy Outlook 2002*, op. cit., pp. 27, 59, 410–11.

28 Energy Information Administration, *Annual Energy Review 2001*, US Department of Energy, Washington, DC, 2002, p. 13.

29 International Energy Agency, *World Energy Outlook 2002*, op. cit., pp. 184–85, 430.

with the stubborn problem of energy poverty, has turned energy consumption into a widely recognised good. Environmentalist John Holdren, who back in the 1970s advocated economic de-development to tame energy consumption, now sees energy as a vital input for economic progress. In his words, 'A reliable and affordable supply of energy is absolutely critical to maintaining and expanding economic prosperity where such prosperity already exists and to creating it where it does not.'[30]

False alarms[31]

The poor track record of critics of the high-energy, carbon-based economy inspires scepticism as regards their sharp turns towards climate alarmism. Some glaring predictive errors by well-known critics have required substantial, albeit reluctant, revision.

After stating in the 1970s, along with John Holdren, that 'it is questionable whether potential resources can be converted into available supplies at economic costs society can pay', Paul Ehrlich admitted in the 1990s that, 'the prices of more raw materials are indeed dropping than are rising'.[32] Ehrlich's conclusion in the 1970s that Los Angeles' smog problem was incompatible with continued reliance on the internal combustion engine was corrected

---

30 John Holdren, 'Memorandum to the President: The Energy-Climate Challenge', in Donald Kennedy and John Riggs (eds), *US Policy and the Global Environment: Memos to the President*, Aspen Institute, Washington, DC, 2000, p. 21. Holdren's earlier views are discussed in Bradley, *Julian Simon*, op. cit., p. 142.

31 See Appendix A to this study. For a critical review of the energy pronouncements of Paul Ehrlich, the father of the modern energy Malthusians, see Bradley, *Julian Simon*, op. cit., pp. 126–49. A critical review of the energy alarms of John Holdren can be found at <http://www.cei.org/pdf/3539.pdf>.

32 Bradley, *Julian Simon*, op. cit., pp. 130–34.

by his acknowledgement in the 1990s of the 'salient success story' of more cars and less pollution.[33] Ehrlich's original concern about global cooling *and* global warming led to a self-correction that global warming was the apparent problem.[34]

Paul Ehrlich's protégé John Holdren, an environmental scientist and energy policy specialist at Harvard University, once feared that the potential death toll from global warming could reach a billion people by 2020.[35] Yet Holdren recently opined: 'That the impacts of global climate disruption may not become the dominant sources of environmental harm to humans for yet a few more decades cannot be a great consolation.'[36] In other signs of retreat or, at least, mixed thoughts, Ehrlich and Holdren have respectively warned against rash policy action based on 'worst-case prognoses'[37] and acknowledged affordable energy as 'the lifeblood of the industrial societies and a prerequisite for the economic development of the others'.[38] All these revisions have been towards *energy and climate realism*, the focus of this study.

Some have suggested that yesterday's alarmists were really 'whistle-blowers' whose 'important early warnings ... averted ... disasters'.[39] But society has been fortunate to have tuned out energy alarmism. Fearing coal depletion, William Stanley Jevons warned

---

33 Ibid., p. 136.

34 Ibid., pp. 144–45.

35 'As [then] University of California physicist John Holdren has said, it is possible that carbon dioxide-induced famines could kill as many as a billion people before the year 2020.' Paul Ehrlich, *The Machinery of Nature*, Simon & Schuster, New York, 1986, p. 274.

36 Holdren, op. cit., p. 23.

37 Bradley, *Julian Simon*, op. cit., pp. 118–19.

38 John Holdren, 'Meeting the Energy Challenge' *Science*, 9 February 2001, p. 945.

39 Richard Norgaard, 'Optimists, Pessimists, and Science', *BioScience*, March 2002, p. 288.

the UK in 1865, 'To allow commerce to proceed until the course of civilization is weakened and overturned is like killing the goose to get the golden egg.'[40] As it turned out, domestic coal supplies were not depleting but expanding in Jevons's lifetime and thereafter before political problems sent the industry into decline. But the UK enjoyed a half-century of energy growth that a hypothetical Bureau of Coal Supply and Allocation could have arrested.

What if the alarms of Paul Ehrlich or John Holdren had inspired a policy of oil rationing and phasing out of the internal combustion engine in the 1970s? What if power plant construction in the USA had been ordered to 'cease immediately ... except in special circumstances', as recommended by Paul Ehrlich and Richard Harriman in 1971?[41] What if the dream of Holdren and Ehrlich in 1973 – 'a massive campaign must be launched to ... de-develop the United States'[42] – had been enacted to control energy usage? A major decarbonisation plan poses the same risk for the UK and EU today.

Relative superiority

Carbon energies are poised to continue to be primary energies for centuries given improving technology *if* political constraints on extraction and combustion are overcome.[43] The carbon energy

---

40 William Stanley Jevons, *The Coal Question: An Inquiry Concerning the Progress of the Nation and the Probable Exhaustion of our Coal Mines*, Macmillan, London, 1865, p. 345.

41 Paul Ehrlich and Richard Harriman, *How to Be a Survivor*, Rivercity Press, Rivercity, MA, 1971, 1975, p. 72.

42 John Holdren, Anne Ehrlich and Paul Ehrlich, *Human Ecology: Problems and Solutions*, W. H. Freeman, San Francisco, CA, 1973, p. 279.

43 Such constraints would include drilling bans in virgin areas and a lack of private property rights to incite exploration and development in many countries around the world. Regulatory disincentives such as well-head price controls can also create artificial scarcity of nature's energy bounty.

age will also continue to dominate because of the economic and environmental problems of today's competing energies. Renewable energy is quantity constrained by *geographical limitations* (geothermal); *siting pressures* (wind and solar farms); on/off *'intermittent'* generation (wind and solar); seasonal and annual *variability* (hydropower); and *prohibitive cost* (on-grid solar). Oil, gas and coal displaced most renewables in the nineteenth century because of greater quantity, density and reliability – all combining for a better product and a better price.[44] These reasons still pertain today.

Hyperbole aside, *renewable technologies are not on a projected path to assume the role that carbon energies have today*.[45] The viability of politically favoured renewables depends in large part on continuing and even accelerating direct government subsidies. This vulnerability was underlined by the editors of *Windpower Monthly* after the World Summit on Sustainable Development in Johannesburg failed to agree to a global renewable quota of 5 per cent by 2010. In their words:

> The doors to potential new markets for wind plant could slam shut … The old markets – Denmark, Germany and Spain – are already stagnating; Denmark's onshore market peaked last year and Germany's is expected to peak this year … The energy market, particularly that for renewable energies, is a political beast, under political control. To secure its future, the wind industry must play politics.[46]

---

44 See Appendix C for the nineteenth-century views of W. S. Jevons on the problems of renewables as primary energy sources.

45 Martin Hoffert et al., 'Advanced Technology Paths to Global Climate Stability: Energy for a Greenhouse Planet', *Science*, 1 November 2002, pp. 983–85.

46 Gail Rajgor and Lyn Harrison, 'Johannesburg Justice', *Windpower Monthly*, July 2002, p. 6.

Nuclear power is not cost competitive with electricity generated using carbon energies in most areas of the world and faces a unique set of political and environmental challenges. If nothing else, the long lead times and large size of nuclear plants limit their attractiveness where carbon energies are available to generate electricity. But nuclear sources remain the only viable carbon-free mass substitute for carbon energy-generated power in the short to medium term, however much environmentalists may not like this fact.

Large-scale renewable projects, other than those using geothermal sources, operate exclusively at the surface of the earth. The diffuse nature of wind and solar power requires collectors that must be spread out over a large area. Carbon energies, by contrast, represent more concentrated forms of energy and require less infrastructure per unit of output. Carbon energies are also more subsurface intensive with drilling and pipeline transport. Since man and nature live at the surface, renewables may be less 'green' than carbon energies under some environmental criteria.[47] This is just one environmental issue that makes *green pricing* for electricity, whereby sellers extract a premium from buyers for environmental considerations, problematic. There is no objective definition of 'green', and real-world trade-offs between environmental objectives make economic differentiation difficult and even suspect.[48]

Conclusion

The carbon energy-dominated energy economy has been improving in virtually every way. Supplies are not depleting but growing

---

47   See Peter Huber, *Hard Green*, Basic Books, New York, 1999, pp. 103–8.
48   Robert Bradley, 'Green Pricing', in John Zumerchik (ed.), *Macmillan Encyclopedia of Energy*, 3 vols, Macmillan, New York, 2000, vol. 2, pp. 598–601.

more abundant. Prices show little sign of systemically increasing net of government energy taxes. Energy usage is rapidly expanding as both the energy rich and the energy poor increase consumption. Energy intensity is falling. Pollution associated with carbon energies have diminished. Blips on the progress screen are more associated with government intervention in markets rather than markets per se, whether it be problems with state-owned oil entities or price controls that create retail shortages.

Much of this progress is anticipated to continue in the next few decades even as the absolute energy consumption and market share of oil, gas and coal are expected to rise. The burden of proof is clearly on the naysayer to show that the *trend*, not a point estimate, is negative; explain why entrepreneurial adjustment cannot be expected to effectively address real problems over time; and differentiate between 'market failure' and the problems caused by government ownership and intervention in markets.

3 ISSUES IN CLIMATE SCIENCE

The environmental debate over the carbon energy economy has changed since the 1970s. Energy usage, once decried as a per se bad, is now recognised as necessary for sustaining the needs of a growing population and for industrialising the developing world. Resource depletion is no longer considered an imminent concern. Air and water pollution are not the problems that they once were, and more improvement is locked in as a result of technology advances and regulatory requirements. Periodic disruptions in the world oil market are subsumed by the persistent overhang of surplus oil. Oil reliability concerns relate to the *government ownership of oil*, not to the commodity itself, which brings the energy problem back to *statism*.[1]

The central energy sustainability issue now concerns the potentially pernicious effects of carbon energy extraction, transportation and combustion on global climate. The current technological/economic inability to *decarbonise* carbon energies[2] makes the energy–climate issue one and the same.

---

1   See the discussion below, pp. 116–18, 143.

2   'Carbon dioxide emissions are the *intended* outcome of oxidising the carbon in the fuel to obtain energy. There is thus no avoiding, or cleaning up, carbon from the fuel source. This perhaps obvious, but often ignored, reality highlights the reason that restraints on carbon dioxide emissions are, by definition, restraints on the use of energy for society. There are thus only three ways to [significantly] reduce carbon emissions: regulate CO_2, raise the price of carbon fuels to discourage use, or offer non-carbon alternatives.' Mark Mills, *A Stunning Regulatory*

The human (anthropogenic) influence on global climate includes (in order of importance):

- Greenhouse gas (GHG) emissions from carbon energy activities that enhance the greenhouse effect to warm the surface and troposphere and cool the stratosphere.[3]
- Sulphate aerosol emissions from coal combustion and other human activity which both cool and warm the planet.
- Deforestation (afforestation) that reduces (increases) carbon intake to increase (diminish) the enhanced greenhouse effect and thus warm (cool) the climate.
- Physical development, which increases temperature through the urban heat island effect.[4]
- Condensation trails (contrails) from aeroplanes, which may minutely warm the surface owing to the formation of cirrus clouds.

An anthropogenic effect on climate (and the biosphere) is inherent in the mass of human activity. The related *sustainability questions* are:

- How much the climate is affected given the *extent*, *distribution* and *timing* of anthropogenic warming.

Burden: EPA Designating CO_2 as a Pollutant, Mills McCarthy & Associates, Chevy Chase, MD, 1998, p. 4. New technological developments over time, however, may allow business-as-usual emissions where the CO_2 is recaptured.

3 An enhanced greenhouse effect reduces the amount of infrared radiation escaping from the lower atmosphere, leaving less radiation to warm the upper atmosphere.

4 The urbanisation effect may be twice as great as previously calculated; see Eugenia Kalnay and Ming Cai, 'Impact of Urbanization and Land-Use Change on Climate', *Nature*, 29 May 2003, pp. 528–31.

- Whether a warmer, wetter[5] world with greater carbon dioxide (CO_2) fertilisation and a higher sea level is region-specific in its effects.
- Whether a prediction of net damages calls for adaptation within a 'no regrets' policy framework or a government-mandated transformation of the energy economy to reduce emissions and/or subsidise the creation of carbon sinks to remove carbon from the atmosphere.

A 'no regrets' policy framework is one in which the impact of GHGs is reduced in a way that leads to no economic cost for any affected group: i.e. leads to a clear Pareto improvement.

Natural and anthropogenic change

James Hansen has stated what can be called the first rule of climate – *inherent change*. In his words: 'Climate is always changing. Climate would fluctuate without any change of [man-made] climate forcing. The chaotic aspect of climate is an innate characteristic.'[6]

Building upon this insight, the US National Research Council has documented how 'large, abrupt climate changes have repeatedly affected much or all of the earth, locally reaching as much as 10°C change in 10 years'.[7] Change, even abrupt change, is not an artefact of the anthropogenic climate-change era but an intrinsic part of climate.

---

5   Warming, natural or anthropogenic, increases evaporation from the oceans to enhance precipitation.

6   James Hansen, 'How Sensitive Is the World's Climate?', *National Geographic Research & Exploration* 9(2), 1993, p. 143.

7   National Research Council et al., *Abrupt Climate Change: Inevitable Surprises*, National Academy Press, Washington, DC, 2002, p. v.

Is there a recognisable human influence on global climate? The IPCC concluded in a 1995 report, 'The balance of evidence suggests a discernible human influence on global climate.'[8] While this finding was controversial upon its release,[9] the appearance of an enhanced greenhouse effect has been increasingly suspected. Even some prominent critics of the IPCC report have noted the distinct distribution profile of warming in the most recent period compared with that in the pre-1945 period, suggesting that the former may well have an anthropogenic component.[10]

The influential 1995 IPCC report concluded that a doubling of the warming potential of greenhouse gases in the atmosphere, estimated to occur by 2100 from 1990 levels, would:

- Raise global temperatures by 2°C (3.6°F), with a range of 1°C to 3.5°C (approximately 2°F to 6°F).
- Increase precipitation by a 'small' but 'potentially intensive' amount.
- Raise sea level by 49 centimetres (19 inches), with a range of 20 to 86 centimetres (8 to 33 inches).[11]

8   John Houghton (ed.), *Climate Change 1995: The Science of Climate Change*, Cambridge University Press, Cambridge, 1996, p. 4. (Henceforth referred to as IPCC, *Climate Change 1995: The Science*.)

9   See Richard Kerr, 'Greenhouse Forecasting Still Cloudy', *Science*, 16 May 1997, pp. 1,040–42.

10 Robert Balling et al., 'Analysis of Winter and Summer Warming Rates in Gridded Temperature Time Series', *Climate Research*, 27 February 1998, pp. 175–81.

11 IPCC, *Climate Change 1995: The Science*, pp. 6, 307–9, 322, 335, 385, 388. The best-guess equilibrium values for a doubling of the warming potential of greenhouse gases in the atmosphere were 2.5°C (4.5°F) for temperature and 150 centimetres (58 inches) for a sea level rise that peaks in the year 2500. An estimated precipitation increase from climate model forecasts for such a doubling of warming potential is 7 per cent with a range between zero and 15 per cent from climate modelling. See Robert Mendelsohn and James Neumann, *The Impact of Climate Change on the United States Economy*, Cambridge University Press, Cambridge, 1999, pp. 11–12.

The report did not suggest a 'greenhouse signal' with weather extremes. 'Overall,' the IPCC concluded, 'there is no evidence that extreme weather events, or climate variability, has increased, in a global sense, through the 20th century, although data and analyses are poor and not comprehensive.'[12] The report reached an ambiguous conclusion as to whether human influence would increase the frequency of droughts and floods. In the IPCC's words, 'A more vigorous hydrological cycle ... translates into prospects for more severe droughts and/or floods in some places and less severe droughts and/or floods in other places.'[13]

The same IPCC report emphasised 'surprises' given the 'unexpected behaviour' of climate inherent in 'the non-linear nature of the climate system ... when rapidly forced'.[14] Examples of such non-linear behaviour 'include rapid circulation changes in the North Atlantic and feedback associated with terrestrial ecosystem changes'.[15] The 'rapid forcing', or high climate sensitivity to GHG concentrations, scenario assumes temperatures in the upper end of the predicted warming range. The possibility of *positive* surprises related to anthropogenic forcing of global climate was not raised in the report, although certain scenarios could be constructed.[16]

12 IPCC, *Climate Change 1995: The Science*, p. 173. See also ibid., pp. 30, 330–31 and 336.

13 Ibid., p. 7. Elsewhere in the Summary for Policymakers (p. 6) is added, 'There is more confidence in temperature projections than hydrological changes.'

14 Ibid., p. 7.

15 Ibid.

16 Anthropogenic warming in the next centuries could cancel out a natural progression towards 'a Little Ice Age', for example. Another example of a positive surprise is the chance that anthropogenic climate change could be *less* apt to disrupt the deep-water thermohaline circulation system in the North Atlantic, a disruption that could trigger rapid global cooling. Carl Wunsch, 'The Ocean and Climate – Separating Myth from Fact', *Marine Technology Journal*, 2 May 1996, pp. 65–68. Communication from Wunsch to author, 19 April 2000.

The 1995 IPCC scientific report noted that global forecasts made by climate models were not yet reliable for predicting localised climate changes. In its words:

> Current climate models lack the accuracy at smaller scales, and the integrations are often too short to permit analysis of local weather extremes. Except maybe for precipitation, there is little agreement between models on changes in extreme events. ... The biases in present day simulations of regional climate change and the inter-model variability in the simulated regional changes are still too large to yield a high level of confidence in simulated change scenarios.[17]

This finding undermines the high-profile predictions of regional climate damage made by the US Global Change Program in 2000.[18] Their report, which calculated net damages for each of five US regions, relied on unduly pessimistic assumptions, used two inconsistent climate models, and discounted the benefits of CO_2 for the biosphere.[19] Richard Kerr of *Science*, commenting on the report, noted that climate models did not have the resolution required to make regional estimates. Those involved in the modelling process, Kerr added, continued to claim that regional resolution was a decade away.[20]

---

17 IPCC, *Climate Change 1995: The Science*, pp. 336, 344. Also see ibid., pp. 41, 43–44 and 46.

18 US Global Change Program, *Climate Change Impacts on the United States: The Potential Consequences of Climate Variability and Change*, Cambridge University Press, Cambridge, 2001.

19 The study used two models with particularly high warming estimates and used the assumption of a 1 per cent annual increase in GHG build-up versus the IPCC recent-year estimate of 0.4 per cent per year.

20 See Richard Kerr, 'Dueling Models: Future US Climate Uncertain', *Science*, 23 June 2000, p. 2,113. This criticism also applies to an IPCC effort to hypothesise the effects of rapid global warming in different regions of the world. Intergovernmental Panel on Climate Change, *The Regional Impacts of Climate Change: An Assessment of Vulnerability*, Cambridge University Press, Cambridge, 1998.

An IPCC reassessment of climate science, released in 2001, re-inforced many of the conclusions of the previous report but made a more confident detection finding. Before, the 'balance of evidence' pointed towards a discernible *greenhouse signal* in the surface temperature record; now the signal was 'very likely' to exist.[21] The sensitivity of global climate to doubled GHG concentrations was unchanged from the 1995 report on the low side (1.5°C (2.7°F)) but increased on the high side from 3.5°C (6.3°F) to 4.5°C (8.1°F). The year 2100 temperature range under different emission scenarios from these sensitivities was widened from a low of 1.4°C (2.5°F) to a high of 5.8°C (10.4°F).[22] A point forecast was not provided in the 2001 report to correspond with the 1995 report's best guess of 2.5°C (4.5°F), but the CO_2 doubling sensitivity for the seven models used for the year 2100 scenarios averaged 2.8°C (5°F).[23]

Media and political attention was drawn to the top of the range, a warming that would be problematic by any standard. Al Gore warned on the home stretch of his campaign for the US presidency in 2000 that 'unless we act, the average temperature is going to go up 10 or 11 degrees [Fahrenheit]'.[24] The editor-in-chief of *Science* rounded the IPCC figures up, describing the 'newest' warming estimate for year 2100 as between 1.5°C and 6.0°C.[25]

As with the prior report, the 2001 reassessment prompted an undertow of discontent in the scientific community. The top

---

21 John Houghton et al., *Climate Change 2001: The Scientific Basis*, Cambridge University Press, Cambridge, 2001, p. 10. (Hereafter cited as IPCC, *Climate Change 2001: The Scientific Basis*.)

22 IPCC, *Climate Change 2001: The Scientific Basis*, p. 13.

23 Ibid., p. 577; IPCC, *Climate Change 1995: The Science*, p. 322.

24 Quoted in Robert Bradley, 'Gore's Tempest Worthy Only of Teapot', *Chicago Sun-Times*, 4 November 2000, p. 18.

25 Don Kennedy, 'New Climate News', *Science*, 10 November 2000, p. 1,091.

estimate of 5.8°C was based on the most extreme of 245 different emission and/or sensitivity scenarios.[26] The best-guess year 2100 temperature calculated from the IPCC multiple scenarios was 2.4°C (4.3°F)[27] – much closer to the bottom than the top of the range and not necessarily a crisis scenario.[28]

A key assumption behind all 245 scenarios, a 1 per cent annual increase in atmospheric concentrations of GHGs, was more than double the observed rate of the last quarter-century. Adjusting the GHG path for the post-1975 growth rate, the 5.8°C top estimate shrinks to 2.6°C for year 2100, with the bottom estimates being about the same.[29]

The latest year 2100 warming estimates are under attack on other grounds as well. A debate has ensued as to whether the IPCC's economic parameters that resulted in high-end emissions and warming were overly pessimistic and resulted from economic parameters that deviated from professional norms.[30]

These controversies aside, Richard Kerr of *Science* reported

26 IPCC, *Climate Change 2001: The Scientific Basis*, pp. 13, 538–40.

27 The 2.4°C (4.3°F) estimate for 1990–2100 warming is calculated from probability estimates in Steve Schneider, 'What Is "Dangerous" Climate Change?', *Nature*, 3 May 2001, pp. 17–19.

28 See below, pp. 69–70.

29 Patrick Michaels et al., 'Revised 21st Century Temperature Projections', *Climate Research*, 20 December 2002, p. 6.

30 For an overview of the 'technically unsound' assumptions in the IPCC scenario analysis, see staff article, 'Hot Potato: The Intergovernmental Panel on Climate Change Had Better Check Its Calculations', *The Economist*, 15 February 2003, p. 72. For the ongoing debate on the eve of the IPCC's fourth assessment, see Ian Castle and David Henderson, 'The IPCC Emission Scenarios: An Economic-Statistical Critique', and Nebojsa Nakicenovic et al., 'IPCC SRES Revisited', *Energy and Environment* 14(2), (3), 2003, pp. 159–85, 187–214; Ian Castle and David Henderson, 'Economics, Emissions Scenarios and the World of the IPCC', *Energy and Environment* 14(4), 2003, forthcoming.

upon the report's release 'a growing appreciation of climate prediction's large and perhaps unresolvable uncertainties'.[31] Indeed, as Kerr discussed, the error bars surrounding the IPCC's estimate of recorded twentieth-century warming and predicted future warming increased, not decreased, as compared with the prior 1995 report. Meanwhile, a definitive link between observed warming and GHG concentrations in the atmosphere still remained uncertain.[32]

Scientific optimism

A closer examination and critical evaluation of the science underlying the IPCC reports permits a non-alarmist – even optimistic – interpretation of the anthropogenic influence on 21st-century climate – and beyond. The latest IPCC report reaches many non-pessimistic conclusions, as discussed below (and presented in Appendix B). Important scientific advances since the 2001 IPCC report, moreover, have moderated the alarm in some important areas, as also discussed below.

As before, the most important problem with alarmism concerns an issue in climate-science methodology – the better-than-nothing, right-until-proven-wrong stature of climate model prediction. These models, out of necessity and not pernicious

---

31 Richard Kerr, 'Rising Global Temperature, Rising Uncertainty', *Science*, 13 April 2001, p. 192.

32 'The uncertainties give some researchers pause when IPCC so confidently attributes past warming to the [enhanced] greenhouse [effect], but projecting warming into the future gives almost everyone the willies … By all accounts, knowledge [about the human role in climate change] will be evolving for decades to come.' Kerr, 'Rising Global Temperature, Rising Uncertainty', op. cit., pp. 192, 194.

design, simplistically derive the all-important feedback effects associated with clouds and water vapour. The result is a large warming bias, and one that cannot be corrected – at least yet – by simply inserting (or permitting the model to calculate) more realistic climate physics.

Millennium warming: more than thought

The 2001 IPCC report concluded, 'The rate and duration of warming of the Northern Hemisphere in the 20th century appears to have been unprecedented during the millennium, and it cannot simply be considered as a recovery from the "Little Ice Age" of the 15th to 19th centuries.'[33] This 'unprecedented' warming has raised concern in two ways. First, the 'hockey stick'[34] estimate of surface temperatures in the last millennium suggests a close correlation between recent warming and accelerating GHG emissions. Second, the temperature jump was prima facie evidence that nature would find it difficult to deal with 'unprecedented' change.

A pair of dual studies published after the 2001 IPCC report found, in the words of a *Science* summary, 'The warming of the 20th century is seen more clearly as a continuation of a trend that began at the start of the 19th century, not the early 20th, and an early period of warmth in the late 10th and 11th centuries is more pronounced than in previous large-scale reconstructions.'[35] This

33 IPCC, *Climate Change 2001: The Scientific Basis*, p. 28.

34 The term 'hockey stick' describes the shape of a well-known millennium temperature record that showed a slow, steady increase in temperatures over 900 years followed by a sharp increase over the last 100 years. See IPCC, *Climate Change 2001: The Scientific Basis*, pp. 133–36.

35 Keith Briffa and Timothy Osborn, 'Blowing Hot and Cold', *Science*, 22 March 2002, p. 2,228.

suggests that natural variability is more pronounced than previously thought, and by inference more of the recent warming could be part of a natural cycle.[36] Another study in *Climate Research* looking at proxy indicators (e.g. tree rings) of temperature change over the last one thousand years found that the twentieth century was not the warmest of the millennium and was not even 'unusually warm or extreme'.[37]

The IPCC's 'likely' conclusion of 'unprecedented warming' is now in doubt – as are the climate models that are calibrated upon the 'hockey stick' global warming conclusion.

Benign warming distribution

The *distribution* of anthropogenic warming is a crucial variable for ascertaining the ecological and economic effects of changing climate. Climate ecologists and economists must determine whether the balance of evidence points towards a *high* and potentially negative warming or a lower and probably positive warming for 2050, 2100 or beyond.

Surface measurements show that minimum (primarily night) temperatures are increasing at twice the rate of

36 For other recent studies on the growing appreciation of natural variability, see Carl Wunsch, 'What Is Thermohaline Circulation?', *Science*, 8 November 2002, pp. 1,179–81; K. S. Carslaw et al., 'Cosmic Rays, Clouds, and Climate', *Science*, 29 November 2002, pp. 1,732–37; G. W. K. Moore et al., 'Climate Change on the North Pacific Region over the Past Three Centuries', *Nature*, 28 November 2002, pp. 401–10; Francisco Chavez et al., 'From Anchovies to Sardines and Back: Multidecadal Change in the Pacific Ocean', *Science*, 10 January 2003, pp. 217–21; Richard Kerr, 'Huge Pacific Waves Trigger Wild Weather Half a World Away', *Science*, 16 May 2003, p. 1,081.

37 Willie Soon and Sallie Baliunas, 'Proxy Climate and Environmental Changes of the Past 1000 Years', *Climate Research*, 21 January 2003, p. 104.

maximum (primarily day) temperatures, creating a decreased diurnal cycle.[38] The enhanced greenhouse signature is also most pronounced in the coldest regions of the world at the coldest times of the year.[39] Rival climate scientists Patrick Michaels and James Hansen have found common ground in debates in which they have presented colour-coded maps showing how the surface GHG warming has been most pronounced in Alaska and Siberia (Hansen) and during the winter (Michaels).[40] This distribution explains why, for example, the increase in surface warmth in the USA is one third below the global average and no greater today than in the 1930s.[41]

The ecological and economic impact of this warming distribution is more benign than a neutral distribution or certainly a reverse distribution, where maximum temperatures would be increasing faster than minimum temperatures. The same is true compared with a scenario in which the warming would be concentrated in populated areas in the warmer months.

Extended period for warming adaptation

The *timing* of warming is also crucial for ascertaining the implica-

---

38 IPCC, *Climate Change 2001: The Scientific Basis*, pp. 2, 4, 33, 101, 104, 106, 108, 129; IPCC, *Climate Change 1995: The Science*, pp. 4, 42, 61, 141, 144–46, 151, 168–69, 172, 201, 290, 294.

39 IPCC, *Climate Change 2001: The Scientific Basis*, pp. 13, 67, 116–17; IPCC, *Climate Change 1995: The Science*, pp. 42, 144.

40 James Hansen et al., 'Climate Forcings in the Industrial Era', *Proceedings of the National Academy of Science*, October 1998, p. 12,756; Balling et al., 'Analysis of Winter and Summer Warming Rates in Gridded Temperature Time Series', op. cit., p. 178.

41 James Hansen et al., 'A Closer Look at United States and Global Surface Temperature Change', *Geophysical Research Letters*, 27 October 2001, p. 23,958.

tions for sustainable development since the slower (faster) the temperature change the more (less) society can naturally adapt. The growth of GHGs in the atmosphere in the last quarter of a century has been linear, not exponential – and well below the 'business-as-usual' estimates of climate models, which assumed growth rates in global warming potential (GWP) of the well-mixed six greenhouse gases as high as 1 per cent per year.[42] These gases, in addition to CO_2, are methane (CH_4), nitrous oxide (N_2O), hydrofluorocarbons (HFCs), perfluorocarbons (PFCs), and sulphur hexafluoride (SF_6).[43]

The IPCC, rejecting the 1 per cent per year composite GHG growth assumption as higher than observed,[44] settle on an average of about 0.65 per cent per year.[45] But the increase in the most recent decade is noted by the IPCC to be 0.4 per cent per year.[46]

In terms of economic impacts and the public policy implications, a GHG growth rate of 0.4 per cent instead of 1 per cent per year would extend the hypothetical doubling time from 70 years to around 150 years. But at a linear growth rate of 1.54 ppmv (parts

42 Michaels et al., 'Revised 21st Century Temperature Projections', op. cit., p. 5; Hansen et al., 'Climate Forcings in the Industrial Era', op. cit., p. 12,758.

43 CO_2 accounts for an estimated 60 per cent of GHG forcing, CH_4 20 per cent, and halocarbons and N_2O about 20 per cent combined. IPCC, *Climate Change 2001: The Scientific Basis*, p. 7.

44 Ibid., p. 527.

45 Ibid., pp. 222–23. This percentage is calculated by the author given a year 2100 value of around 710 ppmv (parts per million volume). Adds Hansen, 'The growth rate of CO_2 (fossil fuel) emissions [as versus CO_2 concentration levels] has declined from about 4 per cent/year to 1 per cent/year in recent decades. It is noteworthy that the current IPCC (2001) scenarios have a growth rate in the 1990s that is almost double the observed rate of 0.8 per cent per year (linear fit to 5-year running mean), but it is consistent with their failure to emphasise data.' James Hansen, 'A Brighter Future', *Climate Change* 52, 2002, p. 437.

46 IPCC, *Climate Change 2001: The Scientific Basis*, p. 7.

per million volume), the post-1974 average,[47] a doubling would take almost 200 years. Such an extension significantly expands the time for natural and human systems to adapt to climate change to both increase benefits and reduce costs in economic terms.

The slowdown of growth of GHG atmospheric concentrations reflects several trends. First, higher CO_2 emissions have been partially offset by increased absorption by plants as biogeochemistry would suggest, an absorption that has been enhanced by the increased precipitation and humidity associated with global warming.[48] Atmospheric concentrations of methane, the second most important GHG, flattened out between 1984 and 1997 before rising again.[49] Radiative chlorofluorocarbons are being phased out and have begun to decrease in the atmosphere.[50]

The future of the carbon cycle is uncertain, but even a return to pre-1975 geometric growth for CO_2 could be below the level currently assumed by the IPCC in its scenario analysis – a compounded yearly increase of 0.65 per cent.

Over-estimated model warming

How sensitive is global climate to man-made increases in atmospheric GHGs? The most direct way to try to answer this question is to compare the *recorded warming* with the *projected* warming.

The GHG build-up and associated global warming potential

---

47 Michaels et al., 'Revised 21st Century Temperature Projections', op. cit., p. 5.
48 Richard Lovett, 'Rain Might Be Leading Carbon Sink Factor', *Science*, 7 June 2002, p. 1,787.
49 E. J. Dlugokencky et al., 'Continuing Decline in the Growth Rate of Atmospheric Methane Burden', *Nature*, 4 June 1998, p. 447; IPCC, *Climate Change 2001: The Scientific Basis*, pp. 248–51.
50 Michaels et al., 'Revised 21st Century Temperature Projections', op. cit., p. 5.

can be measured. If we start an index of GHG concentrations at 100 in 1750, that index would be approximately 152 today, with a weighted average global warming potential (GWP) of 166 versus a model-predicted warming of 200 (a doubling).[51] The recorded surface warming in the last century is around 0.7°C (1.3°F), at least some of which resulted from natural causes given the end of the Little Ice Age in the mid-1800s. Indeed, the surface warming recorded in the first half of the century – about one half of the overall total warming – is likely to have had a prominent non-anthropogenic component.[52]

An upper-range estimate of anthropogenic warming since about the 1880s is 75 per cent of the total recorded surface warming.[53] Other peer-reviewed estimates of the anthropogenic component are as low as 50 per cent.[54] Scaling up an estimated anthropogenic warming from the recorded 66 per cent to a hypothetical 100 per cent would produce a (logarithmic) warming of

---

51 These percentages can be calculated from information provided in IPCC, *Climate Change 2001: The Scientific Basis*, pp. 350–51, 357–58. The fact that an increase in GWP over 60 per cent was not explicit in the report – and reported in the Summary for Policymakers – is peculiar given its importance to the debate.

52 Tom Wigley ('The Science of Climate Change', op. cit., pp. 9–10) attributes the pre-World War II warming primarily to solar factors. Scientific interest in short-term solar forcing continues to reappear (e.g. Richard Kerr, 'The Sun Again Intrudes on Earth's Decadal Climate Change', *Science*, 16 June 2000, p. 1,986; Goddard Institute for Space Studies, 'NASA Study Finds Increasing Solar Trend that Can Change Climate', 20 March 2003).

53 Thomas Crowley, 'Causes of Climate Change over the Past 1000 Years', *Science*, 14 July 2000, p. 276. The latest IPCC report concludes (IPCC, *Climate Change 2001: The Scientific Basis*, p. 10) that 'most' surface warming in the last 50 years was 'likely' to be anthropogenic. This finding, however, is still under debate given recent evidence that natural variability and associated warming were greater than previously believed (see above, pp. 50–51).

54 Judith Lean and David Rind, 'Climate Forcing by Solar Radiation', *Journal of Climate* 11(12), 1998, p. 3,069.

Figure 6   Anthropogenic warming: two estimates

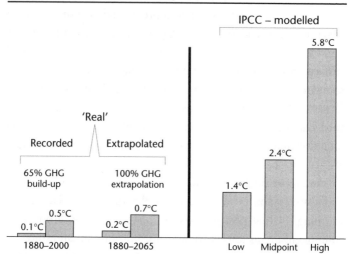

Sources: IPCC, *Climate Change 1995: The Science*, p. 60; IPCC, *Climate Change 2001: The Scientific Basis*, pp. 13, 49, 350, 357; text discussion, pp. 55–6.

well under 1°C (1.8°F) if the doubling occurs between 2060 (IPCC) and 2125 (Michaels).[55] This extrapolation of *factual* warming is substantially below the IPCC estimates for year 2100 warming as seen in Figure 6.[56]

Two major reasons are posited for the apparent over-estimation of model-generated warming. One reason is the alleged cooling offset of sulphate aerosols. It is therefore suggested that

55   IPCC, *Climate Change 2001: The Scientific Basis*, pp. 222–23; Patrick Michaels et al. ('Revised 21st Century Temperature Projections', op. cit.) shows a 2100 estimate of 522 ppmv, which at the linear increase of 1.54 ppmv/year would double the pre-industrial atmospheric GHG levels in around 2125.

56   See p. 48, footnote 27, for the mean estimate from the IPCC scenarios for 1990–2100.

warming caused by other anthropogenic sources may have been greater than overall recorded warming. The 2001 IPCC report opined that the likely net effect was a cooling, offsetting some of the positive greenhouse forcing to explain the lack of net observed surface warming.[57] Yet recent research suggests a close to neutral, even warming, net result from aerosols.[58] A by-product of sulphate aerosol emissions is black carbon or soot. Warming from black carbon 'may nearly balance the net cooling effect of the other anthropogenic aerosol constituents', and, in fact, carbon particulates 'may be the second most important components of global warming after CO_2 in terms of direct forcing'.[59] On the other hand, chemical phenomena that make clouds more reflective may tip the balance of evidence back towards a net neutral-to-cooling effect.[60]

The IPCC has stated, 'the uncertainty in the magnitude of the effect of aerosols on climate is seriously hindering our ability to assess the effect of anthropogenic emissions on climate'.[61] The fourth IPCC scientific assessment, due out in 2007, may well

---

57   IPCC, *Climate Change 2001: The Scientific Basis*, pp. 44–45.

58   'Available data on aerosol single scatter albedo imply that anthropogenic aerosols cause less cooling than has commonly been assumed. ... Our specific conclusion regarding anthropogenic aerosols is that their net "direct" impact on global surface temperature, including "semi-direct" changes of cloud cover, is probably small and even its sign is uncertain.' James Hansen et al., 'Radiative Forcing and Climate Response', *Journal of Geophysical Research*, 27 March 1997, pp. 6,856, 6,861.

59   Mark Jacobson, 'Strong Radiative Heating Due to the Mixing State of Black Carbon in Atmospheric Aerosols', *Nature*, 8 February 2001, p. 695. Also see A. S. Ackerman et al., 'Reduction of Tropical Cloudiness by Soot', *Science*, 12 May 2000, pp. 1,042–47.

60   Robert Charlson et al., 'Reshaping the Theory of Cloud Formation', *Science*, 15 June 2001, pp. 2,025–26.

61   National Research Council, *Aerosol Radiative Forcing and Climate Change*, National Academy Press, Washington, DC, 1996, p. 13.

conclude that sulphates and associated black carbon together do not significantly offset warming. In fact, a new study co-authored by James Hansen reaches this very conclusion.[62] If so, modellers will be under pressure to scale back their sensitivity (warming) estimates to be more in line with actual temperature behaviour.

Another cited reason for the discrepancy between actual and modelled warming is the absorption of heat by the deep oceans, which delays the airborne warming.[63] One major study has confirmed an ocean warming in the period 1948–98 that is broadly consistent with low-sensitivity models. Yet the same study notes that the ocean warming preceded the surface warming, and 'the [ocean] warming could be due to natural variability, anthropogenic effects, or more likely a combination of both'.[64] One subsequent study has concluded that deep ocean temperatures are less a test of model sensitivity than a restatement of the fact that surface temperature influences ocean heat retention.[65] Furthermore, the ocean warmth reflected a temperature jump in 1976/77, called the Great Pacific Climate Shift, an event that is not necessarily tied to greenhouse physics.

The rapid surface warming recorded since the mid-1970s is the strongest indication that the climate model predictions are tracking closer to reality than some sceptics contend. If this trend (0.17°C/decade over the last 25 years) continues (or accelerates),

---

62 Makiko Sato et al., 'Global Atmospheric Black Carbon Inferred from AERONET', *Proceedings of the National Academy of Sciences*, 27 May 2003, pp. 6,319–24.

63 Tim Barnett et al., 'Detection of Anthropogenic Climate Change in the World's Oceans', *Science*, 13 April 2001, pp. 270–74.

64 Sidney Levitus et al., 'Warming of the World Ocean', *Science*, 24 March 2000, p. 2,227.

65 Richard Lindzen, 'Do Deep Ocean Temperature Records Verify Models?', *Geophysical Research Letters*, April 2002, pp. 14,362–65.

model proponents will gain confidence that the IPCC's best guess of climate sensitivity to the enhanced greenhouse effect is robust. Yet this rate of warming is under scrutiny. First, the recent-decade surface warming could be over-estimated by as much as 40 per cent owing to measurement biases over ocean areas.[66] Second, year-to-year global surface temperatures fell in 1999 and again in 2000 from the El Niño-driven high of 1998, although a strong surface-warming trend resumed.[67] Third, atmospheric temperature measurements from satellites suggest a much lower level of GHG-related warming than is inferred by surface temperatures alone, particularly since the 'greenhouse signal', the warming anomaly, should be *greater* in the lower troposphere than at the surface.[68] Figure 7 reveals how two different atmospheric records between 1979 and 2002 show about half the warming that the surface records do and less than half of what the greenhouse signal is supposed to show according to climate models. This empirical anomaly suggests that natural variability is also responsible for recent-decade warming, and climate is less sensitive to GHG forcing than is believed. Fourth, the recent-decade warming is likely to be driven by *both* natural and anthropogenic causes, leaving the anthropogenic component well below the upper end of the climate range. Some of the post-1975 warming, in fact, could well be linked

66 John Christy et al., 'Differential Trends in Tropical Sea Surface and Atmosphere Temperatures since 1979', *Geophysical Research Letters*, 1 January 2001, pp. 183–86. Christy believes that the actual surface warming over the last century is near the bottom of the IPCC range (0.4°C). Personal communication from Christy to author, 15 April 2002.

67 This warming trend is within the 0.15°C/decade range that scientists ranging from 'sceptic' Pat Michaels to 'alarmist' James Hansen have predicted.

68 IPCC, *Climate Change 2001: The Scientific Basis*, pp. 4, 102, 130, 697; National Research Council, *Reconciling Observations of Global Temperature Change*, National Academy Press, Washington, DC, 2000, pp. 2, 70–71.

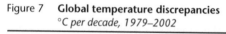

Figure 7   **Global temperature discrepancies**
°C per decade, 1979–2002

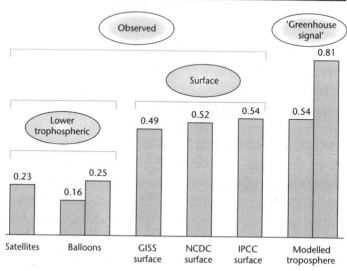

Source: John R. Christy, director, Earth System Science Center, University of Alabama at Huntsville.

to a natural ocean event, the Atlantic Multi-decadal Oscillation.[69] Finally, in terms of public policy implications, the 0.15°C or so decadal trajectory, even if entirely due to anthropogenic causes, is *still* in the lower half of the predicted warming range and arguably economically and ecologically *positive*, as explained below.[70]

Model estimation requires data checks since modelling, at

---

69 Richard Kerr, 'A North Atlantic Climate Pacemaker for the Centuries', *Science*, 16 June 2000, pp. 1,984–86.

70 See pp. 72–5. One has to be careful about the start and end dates of a temperature comparison. For example, a much smaller surface warming was recorded between 1985 and 2001.

best, can provide only a rough approximation of real-world climate. Microphysical climate processes are not well incorporated in climate models owing to limited computing power (even with today's supercomputers) and theoretical unknowns. Any forecast of real-world warming is also imbued with uncertainty because of the multitude of plausible forcing scenarios – natural and anthropogenic. As James Hansen has noted, 'The forcings that drive long-term climate change are not known with an accuracy sufficient to define future climate change.'[71] This is why the 2001 IPCC assessment settled on a wide range from a large multiple scenario analysis rather than a point or best-guess estimate as before. It is also why public policy cannot be reliably anchored to the findings of current climate models.

Water vapour feedback revision

'Feedbacks are what turn the [enhanced] greenhouse effect from a benign curiosity into a potential apocalypse.'[72] The most important – and controversial – driver of high warming estimates in today's climate models concerns feedback from water vapour, the strongest greenhouse gas.[73] A warmer world from man-made GHGs increases evaporation from the surface, primarily oceans. Water molecules trap heat, and water molecules in the upper troposphere where the air is extremely dry trap substantially more heat than those near the surface to 'thicken' the greenhouse. The physics of *fixed relative humidity* in climate modelling throughout

---

71 Hansen, 'Climate Forcings in the Industrial Era', op. cit., p. 12,753.

72 Fred Pierce, 'Greenhouse Wars', *New Scientist*, 19 July 1997, p. 40.

73 IPCC, *Climate Change 2001: The Scientific Basis*, pp. 49, 421.

the atmosphere (rather than just below the cloud level) can *double* the primary warming from anthropogenic GHGs and *magnify* the warming estimates from other forms of feedback with clouds and snow cover. At issue is whether clear-region humidity processes (in the tropics) falsify this key model driver.

Models tend to behave as though relative humidity is fixed at all levels – yet the theoretical and observational basis for such behaviour is highly uncertain (as discussed below). Such model behaviour is less a conspiracy against low-sensitivity outcomes than a result of necessary simplifications, given that modelling complex, real-world climate processes taxes the computational capability of today's models. Models pragmatically veer towards simplicity, yet this simplicity biases their sensitivity finding in an upward direction.[74] If and when climate models become more realistic, their sensitivity findings are likely to be revised downward.

Richard Lindzen has postulated that humidity levels are *decoupled* at the top of the boundary layer, since air above this area is descending.[75] More recently Lindzen has put forward an additional hypothesis: that warming in the tropics from increased radiation causes upper-level cirrus clouds to open to allow the radiation to escape into the atmosphere – an opening akin to the iris of the eye. Precipitation from these cirrus clouds is also a major source of humidity in the tropics. Substituting such physics for model physics makes the IPCC-estimated warming range from doubled CO_2 too high, as seen in Figure 8. The mid-point of Lindzen's range is 1.1°C,

74 See, for example, Gerald North's review of L. D. Danny Harvey's *Global Warming: The Hard Science*, *Climate Change* 49, 2001, p. 495.

75 Richard Lindzen, 'Can Increasing Carbon Dioxide Cause Climate Change?', *Proceedings of the National Academy of Sciences*, August 1997, pp. 8,335–42.

Figure 8   **Warming estimates from doubled GHG forcing**

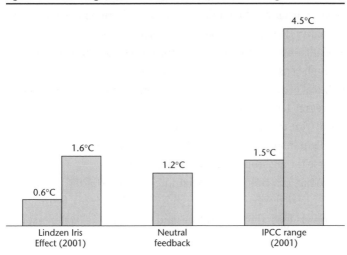

Sources: Richard Lindzen et al., 'Does the World Have an Adaptive Iris?', *Bulletin of the American Meteorological Society*, March 2001, pp. 417–32; IPCC, *Climate Change 2001: The Scientific Basis*, p. 13; text discussion, see pp. 62–3.

a level of warming that corresponds to neutral feedback effects, including with water vapour.

There is interest in Lindzen's hypothesis among feedback specialists, but more observational data is needed before those involved in climate modelling will be forced to begin the arduous work of incorporating a much more complicated set of climate physics. Evidence for Lindzen's wholesale revisionism is under active scrutiny in the scientific journals,[76] a debate

76 Richard Lindzen et al., 'Does the Earth Have an Adaptive Iris?', *Bulletin of the American Meteorological Society*, March 2001, pp. 417–32; D. L. Hartmann et al., 'Tropical Convection at the Top of the Atmosphere', *Journal of Climate*, December 2001, pp. 4,495–511; Ming-Dah Chou et al., 'Comments on "Tropical Convection at the Top of the Atmosphere"', *Journal of Climate*, 1 September 2002,

that could continue for some time. The important point is that even a partially right 'Lindzen effect' would bring model warming estimates down, and even to the low end of the IPCC range. Such a result would not only remove the empirical anomalies created by high-sensitivity climate models. It could also ameliorate the political pressure for near-term GHG emission abatement beyond 'no regret' levels, as defined below.[77] This is because lower climate sensitivity to GHG concentrations not only shrinks the alleged problem but reduces the ability of carbon suppression policies to reverse the anthropogenic effect on climate.

What has been the 'official line' of the IPCC in the face of the crucial feedback controversy? The 1995 report forthrightly acknowledged the importance and challenge of water vapour feedback by concluding:

> Feedback from the redistribution of water vapour remains
> a substantial uncertainty in climate models. ... Intuitive

---

pp. 2,566–70; Q. Fu et al., 'Tropical Cirrus and Water Vapor: An Effective Earth Infrared Iris Feedback?', *Atmospheric Chemistry and Physics*, 30 January 2002, pp. 31–37; M. D. Chou et al., 'Reply to: "Tropical Cirrus and Water Vapor: An Effective Earth Infrared Iris Feedback?"', *Atmospheric Chemistry and Physics*, 30 May 2002, pp. 99–101; Dennis Harmann and Marc Michelson, 'No Evidence for Iris', *Bulletin of the American Meteorological Society*, February 2002, pp. 249–54; Richard Lindzen, 'Comment on "No Evidence for Iris"', *Bulletin of the American Meteorological Society*, September 2002, pp. 1,345–49; Halstead Harrison, 'Comments on "Does the Earth Have an Adaptive Infrared Iris?"', *Bulletin of the American Meteorological Society*, April 2002, pp. 597–99; Thomas Bell et al., 'Reply', *Bulletin of the American Meteorological Society*, April 2002, pp. 598–600; Bing Lin et al., 'The Iris Hypothesis: A Negative or Positive Feedback?', *Journal of Climate*, January 2002, pp. 3–7; Ming-Dah Chou et al., 'Comments on "The Iris Hypothesis: A Negative or Positive Cloud Feedback?"', *Journal of Climate*, 15 September 2002, pp. 2,713–15; Lin Chambers et al., 'Examination of New CERES Data for Evidence of Tropical Iris Feedback', *Journal of Climate*, 15 December 2002, pp. 3,719–26.

77 See below, pp. 119–22.

arguments for [a strong positive feedback] to apply to water vapour in the upper troposphere are weak; observational analysis and process studies are needed to establish its existence and strength.[78]

The 2001 IPCC report did not disavow its earlier scepticism but raised a challenge for Lindzen and other sceptics of a strong positive water vapour feedback:

> For a challenge to the current view of water vapour feedback to succeed, relevant processes would have to be incorporated into a GCM, and it would have to be shown that the resulting GCM accounted for observations at least as well as the current generation [of models]. A challenge to meet this test has not emerged.[79]

Putting the burden of proof on real-world complexity rather than model simplicity, the 2001 report concluded, 'The balance of evidence favours a positive clear-sky water vapour feedback of magnitude comparable to that found in simulations.'[80]

Perhaps the most important question of the climate debate is how much longer the benefit of the doubt will go to the current models given the chasm of theoretical uncertainty and the open secret that models cannot simulate complex climate processes. The next IPCC scientific assessment can be expected to focus squarely on feedback magnification of global warming with virtually any Iris Effect (or substitute mechanism) reducing the current estimated range of warming caused by a doubling of CO_2 concentrations, which is currently 1.5–4.5°C.

---

78   IPCC, *Climate Change 1995: The Science*, pp. 161–62, 210.
79   IPCC, *Climate Change 2001: The Scientific Basis*, p. 427.
80   Ibid., p. 427.

Moderated forecast of sea level rise

The IPCC's best-guess forecast of sea level rise, first presented in 1990, was reduced by 25 per cent in the IPCC report in 1995.[81] The new estimate was reduced a further 2 per cent in the 2001 IPCC report.[82] Yet as with temperature, a discrepancy between *model-estimated* sea level rise and *recorded* sea level rise suggests model over-estimation. The forecast of anthropogenic sea level rises from a doubling of greenhouse gases in the atmosphere by 2100 is 48 centimetres (18.5 inches), with a range of 9 to 88 centimetres (3.5 to 34 inches).[83] This climate-model forecast compares with an actual increase in the last century of 15 centimetres (5.9 inches).[84] Some of this rise occurred before mid-century when natural variability was the controlling factor, continuing a trend from previous centuries and even millennia.[85] The anthropogenic portion of sea level rise, like the temperature portion, suggests that the IPCC-estimated range is biased on the high side. In any case, sea level rise has not accelerated in recent decades,[86] suggesting that other factors rather than GHG build-up are at work.

Melting ice, a potential contributor to sea level rise, has been a particularly well-publicised aspect of the climate debate. An arctic thinning in 1998/99 sounded alarms, but by 2002 most of the change had been reversed.[87] The front page of *The New York Times* in August 2000 reported that an 'unprecedented' patch of ocean

---

81 IPCC, *Climate Change 1995: The Science*, p. 6.
82 IPCC, *Climate Change 2001: The Scientific Basis*, p. 16.
83 Ibid., p. 642.
84 Ibid., p. 641.
85 Ibid.
86 Ibid., p. 31.
87 Richard Kerr, 'Whither Arctic Ice? Less of It, for Sure', *Science*, 30 August 2002, p. 1,491. Wind shifts, called the Arctic Oscillation (AO), appear to be responsible for changing ice levels, not just absolute temperature changes. Yet, 'currently, there

water was witnessed around the ice at the North Pole. Scientific criticism led to a retraction ten days later. Such open water was not unprecedented, and if it had been, the observed phenomenon was not necessarily anthropogenic.[88] Indeed, temperature records in the Arctic failed to indicate surface warming that then could be linked to anthropogenic melting.[89] Overall, West Antarctica has slightly thinned (continuing a very long trend), and East Antarctica has not thinned in recent decades.[90] Some important Alaska points show ice thickening even with a surface temperature warming.[91]

While arctic melting would not affect sea level rise in a major way (just as melting an ice cube in a glass of water does not raise its water level), a melting of Antarctica's Greenland Ice Sheet, which lies on land above sea level, would. Yet a pair of studies of the ice sheet found 'no net reduction in ice volume, with a substantial thickening in the south-west balanced by thinning in the south-east'.[92] Warming was melting ice at the

is no generally accepted theory for the existence of the AO'. Richard Moritz et al., 'Dynamics of Recent Climate Change in the Arctic', *Science*, 30 August 2002, p. 1,499.

88 John Wilford, 'Ages-Old Icecap at North Pole is Now Liquid, Scientists Find', *New York Times*, 19 August 2000, p. A1; John Wilford, 'Open Water at Pole is Not Surprising, Experts Say', *New York Times*, 29 August 2000, p. D3.

89 Roman Przybylak, 'Temporal and Spatial Variation of Surface Air Temperature over the Period of Instrumental Observations in the Arctic', *International Journal of Climatology* 20, 2000, pp. 587–614.

90 Charles Raymond, 'Ice Sheets on the Move', *Science*, 13 December 2002, pp. 2,147–48; Eric Rignot and Robert Thomas, 'Mass Balance of Polar Ice Sheets', *Science*, 30 August 2002, pp. 1,502–5.

91 G. W. K. Moore et al., 'Climate Change on the North Pacific Region over the Past Three Centuries', *Nature*, 28 November 2002, pp. 401–10; Francisco Chavez, et al., 'From Anchovies to Sardines and Back', op. cit., p. 217.

92 Dorthe Dahl-Jensen, 'The Greenland Ice Sheet Reacts', *Science*, 21 July 2000, p. 404. The two studies were published in the same issue of *Science*. Also see Richard Alley, 'On Thickening Ice?', *Science*, 18 January 2002, pp. 451–52; Kenneth Chang, 'The Melting (Freezing) of Antarctica', *New York Times*, 2 April 2002, pp. D1–D2.

fringes, but greater precipitation from increased evaporation of the oceans was adding ice to the interior – an offset or 'negative feedback' that moderates this aspect of the climate alarm.

Increased weather extremes – unconfirmed

The data to date – after over a century of GHG build-up in the atmosphere – does not confirm the contention that human influence will increase weather extremes. As was found in 1995, the latest IPCC report concludes that available data does not show an increase in the frequency of hurricanes, tornadoes, thunder days, hail, or El Niño events.[93] The possibility of non-linear 'surprises' is mentioned, but 'a large degree of uncertainty about the mechanisms involved' precludes further treatment.[94] Furthermore, differentiation between positive and negative 'rapid and irreversible changes in the climate system' is not made.[95]

Regarding weather extremes over the next century, the IPCC notes that model forecasting is severely limited 'due to the fact that ... severe weather phenomenon are sub-grid scale' and 'there remains uncertainty with respect to the governing mechanisms'.[96] Hints about 'an emerging common signal'[97] of increased 21st-century storminess, however, beg the question of climate sensitivity to GHG forcing, itself in dispute, as argued in this paper.

---

93   IPCC, *Climate Change 2001: The Scientific Basis*, pp. 5, 15–16, 33–34 and 104.

94   Ibid., p. 53.

95   Ibid.

96   Ibid., p. 573.

97   Ibid.

Deep distant warming: still a false alarm?

The maturing carbon energy age makes it virtually a foregone conclusion that a doubling of pre-industrial atmospheric GHG concentrations will be reached this century. It also makes a tripling of such concentrations plausible in the next century. Yet a tripling scenario is not necessarily problematic for two reasons. First, atmospheric CO_2 concentrations will move closer to a biosphere optimum, as discussed below.[98] Second, climate sensitivity to GHGs *decreases* with increasing GHG concentrations. In technical terms, the climate effect grows disproportionately smaller as greenhouse gas concentrations rise owing to the properties of carbon dioxide absorptivity at infrared wavelength.[99]

The estimated warming effect from a doubling of GHG concentrations assuming neutral feedback effects is 1.2°C. The effect of a *quadrupling* of GHG concentrations will be only double this level, as seen in Figure 9 for the neutral feedback scenario, just as for the IPCC midpoint-warming scenario (which, as argued above, is likely to be revised downward in the future). The 'threshold value' in the middle is an estimate of problematic warming for comparison.

While this relationship is less extreme than a linear GHG–temperature relationship would be, anthropogenic climate change would still increase under a base-level forcing scenario. Yet it is highly uncertain what the atmospheric concentration of CO_2

---

98 See pp. 73–5.

99 For an explanation of the logarithmic (not linear) relationship, see Horace Byers, *General Meteorology*, McGraw-Hill, New York, 1974, p. 32. For discussion of this effect for economic benefit/cost, see William Nordhaus and Joseph Boyer, *Warming the World: Economic Models of Global Warming*, MIT Press, Cambridge, MA, 2000, p. 142. Also see the discussion in IPCC, *Climate Change 2001: The Scientific Basis*, p. 534.

Figure 9   **Atmospheric GHG build-up and warming**

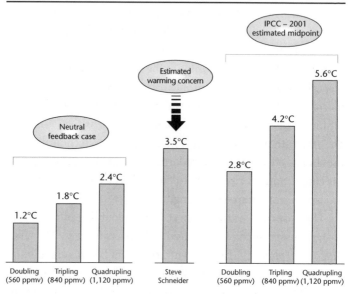

Sources: IPCC, *Climate Change 1995: The Science*, p. 60; Steve Schneider, 'What Is "Dangerous" Climate Change?', *Nature*, 3 May 2001, pp. 17–19; IPCC, *Climate Change 2001: The Scientific Basis*, p. 577; text discussion, p. 69.

will be in the next century and beyond owing to unknowns regarding the rate of carbon emissions and natural carbon sequestration. New technological developments affecting emission and sequestration later in the century magnify the uncertainty. Extrapolating warming trends to future centuries (2100 and beyond) is highly speculative for climate prediction and cost–benefit analysis since the range of forcing scenarios and other unknowns is so wide. The atmospheric concentration of greenhouse gases could be virtually any level desired in such a distant, technologically richer future. The case for climate alarmism and policy activism appears to be no stronger for the next century than for the present one.

Conclusion

Climate alarmism is based on a number of debatable postulations that must stretch into the very distant future. A non sequitur that runs throughout is that human influence on climate cannot be good but only bad. Yet there are a number of reasons to view the human influence on climate *optimistically* given the direction of warming, the favourable distribution of the supposed 'greenhouse signal', and the lack of theoretical and empirical evidence for an increase in weather extremes. This said, the most important development to defeat climate alarmism may well be in the making right now – a reconsideration of the mainstream view of the magnification of warming from feedback effects.

The *balance of evidence*, a term used to link human influence to climate in the 1995 IPCC scientific report, can be employed to make a more important point: *the balance of evidence leans more towards climate optimism than climate pessimism*. But an optimistic conclusion does not simply rely on an analysis of climatology. It follows from the ability of technology and economic wealth in free-market settings to create the best outcomes from a climate that is always in flux for natural and man-made reasons.

4 ISSUES IN CLIMATE ECONOMICS

Climate economics, a relatively new branch of applied economics, translates the findings of climatology into economic terms to inform the public policy debate. Man-made changes in climate, and market responses, confer social benefits and costs (non-priced externalities) and are part of the sustainability debate. Government policy in response to the climate issue has its own costs and benefits; it too is part of the sustainability debate. These economic estimates must be discounted to the present, which magnifies near-term costs relative to longer-term benefits. In comparing future economic effects, all roads start from what is perhaps the most scientifically anchored fact in the climate debate – the positive role of carbon dioxide fertilisation in planetary productivity.

Carbon dioxide – a *positive* GHG

Carbon dioxide (CO_2) is the most important anthropogenic greenhouse gas. It has less forcing properties than methane (CH_4) but lasts far longer in the atmosphere. In terms of recorded global warming potential associated with emissions between 1750 and today, CO_2 constitutes 60 per cent of the basket of man-made greenhouse gases.[1]

---

1   See p. 53, footnote 43.

CO_2, a natural by-product of the modern energy economy, has *known* positive properties. It is not a pollutant but a building block of a living and vibrant biosphere.[2] There is a positive relationship between airborne carbon dioxide concentrations and plant growth and productivity. Plant respiration, water-use efficiency, and the ability to handle weather stress are enhanced by elevated CO_2 in the amounts experienced or projected in the carbon energy age.[3] As CO_2 concentrations rise, the temperature optimum for most plants increases as well.[4]

The optimum atmospheric CO_2 level for biosphere productivity from enhanced photosynthesis has been estimated at between 800 and 1,200 parts per million volume (ppmv).[5] At such a level, experiments indicate that plant growth is stimulated to maximise vegetative and biological productivity, other things remaining the same.

The mid-point of 1,000 ppmv can be compared with today's estimated level of 375 ppmv and two projected levels by 2100: using the most recent 25-year average increase (1.54 ppmv per year) leading to a projected level of 522 ppmv and the IPCC-projected increase to approximately 715 ppmv.[6] An unhealthy CO_2 level for humans is around 15,000 ppmv, which is conceivable inside a deep coal mine but not out in the open air.[7] Figure 10

---

2 Unlike the US Clinton administration, the Bush administration has been careful to label CO_2 as an emission and not a pollutant in its discourse on the subject.

3 Sylvan Wittwer, *Food, Climate, and Carbon Dioxide: The Global Environment and World Food Production*, Lewis Publishers, New York, 1995, pp. 89–91.

4 New Hope Environmental Services, *In Defense of Carbon Dioxide*, Greening Earth Society, New Hope, VA, 1998, p. 7.

5 Wittwer, op. cit., pp. 89–91.

6 IPCC, *Climate Change 2001: The Scientific Basis*, pp. 185, 222. The IPCC figure for 1999 of 367 ppmv is increased by 0.4 per cent for three years to give a current estimate.

7 New Hope Environmental Services, op. cit., pp. 1–2.

Figure 10   **Atmospheric CO₂ levels and social welfare**
Parts per million by volume

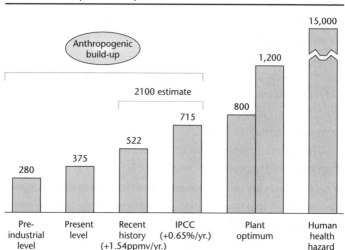

Sources: IPCC, *Climate Change 1995: The Science*, pp. 21–26; Sylvan Wittwer, *Food, Climate, and Carbon Dioxide*, CRC Press, Boca Raton, FL, 1995, pp. 89–91; New Hope Environmental Services, *In Defense of Carbon Dioxide*, Greening Earth Society, New Hope, VA, 1998, p. 1.

shows the current and projected atmospheric CO_2 concentrations, an estimated optimum range for plants and the threshold where inhalation negatively impacts on human health.

Today's CO_2 level, approximately one third greater than in the mid-nineteenth century, is estimated to have increased plant and crop biomass and productivity in the agriculture and forestry sectors by between 5 and 10 per cent.[8] Eight researchers reported in *Science* that terrestrial net primary production increased by over 6 per cent between 1982 and 1999, a period when atmospheric CO_2

---

8   Wittwer, op. cit., p. 86.

concentrations increased by 9 per cent, with positive results in all regions of the world.[9] Carbon fertilisation and related anthropogenic effects are one reason why global food production is at an all-time high.[10]

A doubling of CO_2 from today's estimated level of 375 ppmv is expected to increase biomass and economic yield by 10 per cent for C_4 plants like corn and sugar cane, and as much as 33 per cent for C_3 plants like rice, wheat, potatoes and vegetables.[11] This fertilisation effect could also spur undesirable plant growth and pest populations,[12] problems that improving technology can be expected to address.

Continued carbon energies usage in future centuries could bring atmospheric CO_2 levels into the optimum range. The climate effects (warmer nights, increased precipitation) associated with such elevated CO_2 concentration would have benefits for plant growth and productivity as well.

IPCC damage analysis versus mainstream economics

The IPCC is best known for its scientific studies on climate change, published as the first assessment in 1990, volume I of the three-volume second assessment in 1995, and volume I of the

9   Ramakrishna Nemani et al., 'Climate-driven Increases in Global Terrestrial Net Primary Production from 1982 to 1999', *Science*, 6 June 2003, pp. 1,560–63.

10   Indur Goklany, 'Potential Consequences of Increasing Atmospheric CO_2 Concentration Compared to Other Environmental Problems', *Technology* 75, 2000, pp. 191–92.

11   Wittwer, op. cit., p. 90. C_3 and C_4 species are categorised by their photosynthetic pathways with the C_3 species representing about 95 per cent of the earth's plants (ibid., p. 64).

12   Sir John Houghton, *Global Warming – the Complete Briefing*, Cambridge University Press, Cambridge, 1997, pp. 124–26.

three-volume third assessment in 2001. The two other concurrent reports released in 1995 and 2001 focused on the impacts of anthropogenic climate change, technology and the public policy issues therein. The non-climate science reports have been relatively controversial because uncertain economic analysis has been layered upon uncertain scientific analysis, and the author group has been dominated by government bureaucrats and policy activists rather than more impartial academics.

1995 IPCC report: *Economic and Social Dimensions*

Volume III of the 1995 IPCC report, *Economic and Social Dimensions of Climate Change*, called for policy activism based on the authors' interpretation of the scientific findings of Volume I and their own social science research. The report recommended action based on 'significant "no regrets" opportunities [that] are available in most countries'. But it went much farther by concluding, 'the risk of aggregate net damage due to climate change, consideration of risk aversion, and application of the precautionary principle provide rationale for action beyond no regrets'.[13] How was this jump made to policy activism beyond no regrets?

Chapter 6 of this report, 'The Social Costs of Climate Change: Greenhouse Damages and the Benefits of Control', provided a 'best guess' damage estimate from a doubling of greenhouse gases in the atmosphere assuming a 2°C (3.6°F) warming and associated precipitation and sea level rise. The costs were estimated at 1.5–2 per cent of world GDP, 1–1.5 per cent of developed country

---

13 Intergovernmental Panel on Climate Change, *Climate Change 1995: Economic and Social Dimensions of Climate Change*, Cambridge University Press, Cambridge, 1996, p. 5. (Hereafter cited as *Economic and Social Dimensions: 1995*.)

GDP, and 2–9 per cent of developing country GDP. Longer-term warming damage was estimated to increase less than linearly, an example being a global 6 per cent GDP loss from a temperature increase of 10°C (18°F).[14]

The above analysis – and call for policy activism – was criticised for severely over-estimating future costs and under-estimating future benefits of a business-as-usual world. 'In the area of damages and impacts perhaps more than in the others,' complained William Nordhaus, 'there is a strong tendency to see the cloud behind every silver lining; much analysis, particularly by environmentally oriented researchers, has focused on the damages and ignored the potential benefits of climate change.'[15]

Part of the cost inflation resulted from the report's implicit assumptions of increasing weather extremes, negative surprises and specific regional effects – three drivers that were not established in Volume I on climate science but assumed in the 900-page Volume II report, *Impacts, Adaptation and Mitigation of Climate Change: Scientific-Technical Analysis*[16] and the aforementioned Volume III. Benefits were understated by downplaying the positive role of CO_2 and a warmer and wetter climate as shown by bottom-up, sector-by-sector analysis.[17] The IPCC in Volume III was also

---

14 IPCC, *Economic and Social Dimensions: 1995*, p. 218. The high-end scenario was well outside the range of IPCC-predicted warming in the scientific volume of the second assessment.

15 William Nordhaus, 'Assessing the Economics of Climate Change', in Nordhaus (ed.), *Economics and Policy Issues in Climate Change*, Resources for the Future, Washington, DC, 1998, p. 20.

16 Intergovernmental Panel on Climate Change, *Climate Change 1995: Impacts, Adaptation and Mitigation of Climate Change*, Cambridge University Press, Cambridge, 1996, pp. 3–5, 23–25.

17 This refers to the work of Robert Mendelsohn, discussed below, pp. 88–90.

agnostic towards assigning a realistic discount rate to compare future benefits with present costs.[18]

Volume III, a 450-page study, also ignored the *politicisation problem*;[19] that is, it failed to take into account the problem of government failure replacing market failure. What institutions and incentives might be necessary for a major international effort to effectively transfer benefits from the present to the future to mitigate the alleged intergenerational effects of negative man-made climate change? What problems might governmental institutions encounter in terms of imperfect knowledge, conflicts, gaming and fraud? There was no consideration of public choice and institutional economics related to the climate change issue – an area that is important for the policy debate – in the IPCC report.[20]

2001 IPCC report: *Impacts, Adaptation, and Vulnerability*

Volume II of the 2001 assessment, *Climate Change 2001: Impacts, Adaptation, and Vulnerability*, continued the IPCC's divergence from mainstream economics and climate science.[21] Worst-case

---

18 The authors consider a 'normative' or 'ethical' discount rate as equally valid as a traditional discount measure. See Kenneth Arrow et al., 'Intertemporal Equity, Discounting, and Economic Efficiency', in IPCC, *Economic and Social Dimensions: 1995*, pp. 129–44.

19 See the discussion below, pp. 94–6.

20 For an introduction to public choice theory, see Gordon Tullock, 'Public Choice', in John Eatwell et al. (eds), *The New Palgrave: A Dictionary of Economics*, Palgrave Publishers, New York, 1998, pp. 1,040–44. For a public choice interpretation of the climate debate, see Bruce Yandle, 'Bootleggers, Baptists, and Global Warming', *PERC Policy Series*, PS-14, Political Economy Research Center, November 1998.

21 Intergovernmental Panel on Climate Change, *Climate Change 2001: Impacts, Adaptation, and Vulnerability*, Cambridge University Press, Cambridge, 2001.

scenarios suggested in the IPCC science summary became the focus of analysis, and negative regional impacts were confidently predicted.

The Summary for Policymakers opined, 'Projected climate changes during the 21st Century have the potential to lead to future large-scale and possibly irreversible changes in Earth systems resulting in impacts at continental and global scales.'[22] What could lead to this? 'Examples include significant slowing of the ocean circulation that transports warm water to the North Atlantic, large reductions in the Greenland and West Antarctic Ice Sheets, accelerated global warming due to carbon cycle feedbacks in the terrestrial biosphere, and releases of terrestrial carbon from permafrost regions and methane from hydrates in coastal sediments.' The summary describes these scenarios as 'not well known' and having a 'very low' likelihood but concludes that their probability increases with GHG atmospheric concentrations.[23] What was not mentioned was that these events, which all have historical precedents, are not necessarily linked to GHG forcing and in some cases could be negatively correlated. Nor is there mention of any potential of *positive* surprise scenarios such as GHG forcing acting as protection against the onset of a little ice age for the next several hundred years.

The 1,000-page report failed to consider alternative cases based on an optimistic view of future climate, one that could be developed from conclusions of the science as presented above and in the IPCC's own words as set out in Appendix B. The only concession made to non-alarmists was the recognition that 'human and

22   Ibid., p. 6.
23   Ibid.

natural systems will to some degree adapt autonomously to climate change', and further 'planned' adaptation would be necessary as well.[24] Part of this repetition from the earlier (1995) report reflected a policy decision on the part of the IPCC government representatives that an updated cost–benefit investigation would be secondary to policy actions requiring reduced GHG emissions.[25] Perhaps this is why such an authority as Robert Mendelsohn, one of the world's leading microclimate economists, whose documentation of the positive side of the human influence on climate is described below, was not invited to participate in drafting the 2001 report.[26]

Kyoto modelling studies

In 1998/99 the Stanford Energy Modeling Forum convened thirteen modelling teams, half from the USA and the rest from abroad, to model and run variants of three scenarios: economic and energy business-as-usual; Kyoto compliance under varying assumptions; and atmospheric GHG concentration paths to 550 ppmv.[27] Widely varying estimates of the cost of Kyoto resulted from the disparate treatment of three major unknowns: international CO_2 trading, credit for carbon sinks and the five non-CO_2 greenhouse gases, and post-2010 levels of emission reduction commitments.

The editors of a volume of papers containing the modelling results reached three general conclusions:

---

24   Ibid., p. 8.

25   Lomborg, op. cit., p. 301.

26   Communication from Robert Mendelsohn to author, 12 February 1999.

27   John Weyant and Jennifer Hill, 'Introduction and Overview' to 'The Costs of the Kyoto Protocol: A Multi-Model Evaluation', *Energy Journal*, special issue, International Association for Energy Economics, 1999, pp. vii, xiii, xix.

First, meeting the requirements of the Kyoto Protocol will not stop economic growth anywhere in the world, but it will not be free either. In most Annex 1 countries, significant adjustments will need to be undertaken and cost will need to be paid. Second, unless care is taken to prevent it, the sellers of international emissions rights (dominantly the Russian Federation in the case of Annex 1 trading, and China and India in the case of global trading) may be able to exercise market power raising the cost of the protocol to the other Annex 1 countries. Third, meaningful global trading probably requires that the non-Annex countries take on emissions targets; without them accounting and monitoring (even Annex 1 monitoring and enforcement may be quite difficult) becomes almost impossible. Finally, it appears that the emissions trajectory prescribed in the Kyoto Protocol is neither optimal in balancing the costs and benefits of climate change mitigation, nor cost effective in leading to stabilization of the concentration of carbon dioxide at any level above about 500 ppmv.[28]

Annex 1 countries are those that agreed under the UN Framework Convention on Climate Change to stabilise carbon emissions at their 1990 levels by 2000. They include the OECD countries and countries of the former Soviet bloc. While a lone paper concluded that the costs of compliance with the Kyoto Protocol would be substantially less for the USA than for Europe,[29] the other articles

---

28 Ibid., p. xliv.

29 Warwick McKibbin et al., 'Emission Trading, Capital Flows and the Kyoto Protocol,' in 'The Costs of the Kyoto Protocol: A Multi-Model Evaluation', *Energy Journal*, special issue, International Association for Energy Economics, 1999, pp. 287–333. This model's very low marginal costs estimate – and estimated carbon tax needed to correct the perceived externality – reflects highly optimistic assumptions about technological change and substitution to low-carbon capital. See John Weyant, 'An Introduction to the Economics of Climate Change Policy', Pew Center on Global Climate Change, July 2000, pp. 36–38.

reached the opposite conclusion and described other troubling implications of the protocol:

- US compliance with Kyoto could be achieved at a carbon price of $26 per ton with full international trading and $250 per ton without trading.[30]
- 'With each passing year the difficulty of meeting any fixed quantitative target increases progressively … Sooner or later … the Kyoto targets will need to be reconsidered.'[31]
- Even assuming Annex 1 trading, the net present cost of Kyoto compliance for all signatories is $716 billion, two-thirds of which is borne by the USA, with a cost–benefit ratio of 1:7.[32]
- 'The emission reduction targets as agreed in the Kyoto Protocol are irreconcilable with economic rationality. … With so many open questions, some of which call for a research programme of years, one may wonder whether the great haste with which policy makers agree to international treaties is a sensible strategy.'[33]
- 'Given the projections for emissions in the baseline and the policy variants as simulated with the WorldScan model,

30 Christopher MacCracken et al., 'The Economics of the Kyoto Protocol', in 'The Costs of the Kyoto Protocol: A Multi-Model Evaluation', op. cit., p. 25.

31 Henry Jacoby and Ian Sue Wing, 'Adjustment Time, Capital Malleability and Policy Cost', in 'The Costs of the Kyoto Protocol: A Multi-Model Evaluation', op. cit., p. 91.

32 William Nordhaus and Joseph Boyer, 'Requiem for Kyoto: An Economic Analysis', in 'The Costs of the Kyoto Protocol: A Multi-Model Evaluation', op. cit., p. 93.

33 Richard Tol, 'Kyoto, Efficiency, and Cost-Effectiveness: Applications of FUND', in 'The Costs of the Kyoto Protocol: A Multi-Model Evaluation', op. cit., pp. 131, 154.

the Kyoto targets do not reflect an efficient distribution of emission reductions.'[34]

- The marginal cost of Kyoto compliance in 2010 for the USA without trading is $153 per ton and with trading is under $40 per ton. In the trading case, the USA is the world's leading purchaser of carbon credits with supply coming mostly from eastern Europe and the former Soviet Union.[35]

- 'Emissions trading has significant potential to improve welfare for all parties, [but] … exercise of market power is clearly possible under policies like Annex 1 trading that create markets with a single seller.'[36]

- 'The projected economic impacts (GDP, GNP, consumption) on Australia and the United States are higher than for Japan and the European Union. This is because, although the size of the carbon penalty is important in determining the economic impacts of emission abatement, the extent to which a particular country relies on fossil fuels in the production structure or its economy is also important.'[37]

- 'The impact of meeting the Kyoto emissions targets by 2010 and then holding emissions at those levels thereafter means that the resulting loss of potential output increases gradually

34 Johannes Bollen et al., 'Clubs, Ceilings and CDM: Macroeconomics of Compliance with the Kyoto Protocol', in 'The Costs of the Kyoto Protocol: A Multi-Model Evaluation', op. cit., p. 199.
35 Mikiko Kainuma et al., 'Analysis of Post-Kyoto Scenarios: The Asian-Pacific Integrated Model', in 'The Costs of the Kyoto Protocol: A Multi-Model Evaluation', op. cit., pp. 218–19.
36 Paul Bernstein et al., 'Effects of Restrictions on International Permit Trading: The MS-MRT Model', in 'The Costs of the Kyoto Protocol: A Multi-Model Evaluation', op. cit., p. 255.
37 Vicek Tulpulé et al., 'The Kyoto Protocol: An Economic Analysis using GTEM', in 'The Costs of the Kyoto Protocol: A Multi-Model Evaluation', op. cit., p. 274.

over time – for example, for the US from 2.5 per cent in 2010 to 4.2 per cent by 2020.'[38]

- 'From a welfare perspective, the major effect of the Kyoto agreement is to produce a large wealth transfer from [Annex 1] to the Non [Annex 1], while realizing none of the potential benefits of CO_2 control.'[39]

The US Congress turned to the Energy Information Administration (EIA) for an estimate of the impacts of carbon reduction on the US economy. The EIA modelled six GHG emission reduction scenarios ranging from Kyoto compliance (1990 levels minus 7 per cent by 2010) to 1990 levels plus 24 per cent by 2010. Compared with the 'reference' business-as-usual case (1990 levels plus 36 per cent for 2010), total energy consumption was projected to fall by 18 per cent with energy intensity forced from 1 per cent to 3 per cent per annum. This result would be driven by a \$348 per ton carbon price (tax) that would increase electricity prices by 86 per cent and petrol prices by 53 per cent above the reference case. GDP was estimated to be 4.2 per cent lower by 2010 as well.[40]

---

38 Adrian Cooper et al., 'The Economic Implications of Reducing Carbon Emissions: A Cross-Country Quantitative Investigation Using the Oxford Global Macroeconomic and Energy Model', in 'The Costs of the Kyoto Protocol: A Multi-Model Evaluation', op. cit., p. 349.

39 Stephen Peck and Thomas Teisberg, 'CO_2 Emissions Control Agreements: Incentives for Regional Participation', in 'The Costs of the Kyoto Protocol: A Multi-Model Evaluation', op. cit., p. 390. The Annex 1 countries are developed countries, all of which approved the Kyoto Protocol in 1997. See below, p. 100.

40 US Energy Information Administration, *Impacts of the Kyoto Protocol on US Energy Markets and Economic Activity*, October 1998, p. xv. The EIA study was peer-reviewed by energy specialists at Hagler Bailly Services, Harvard University, Resources for the Future, Stanford University Modeling Forum, and Yale University.

Several key assumptions contributed to the estimates of sizeable costs. First, a start date of 2005 towards compliance by 2010 was assumed, although earlier capital decisions were modelled. (The Kyoto agreement stipulated that demonstrable progress be made by 2005.) Second, the results did not assume domestic or international carbon trading owing to the unspecified international framework and difficulties of monitoring and compliance.[41]

A new simulation run by EIA's National Energy Modeling System the next year changed the start date to 2000 from 2005. This reduced the carbon price and moderated the rise in power and gasoline costs by about 10–15 per cent, and the GDP loss was significantly reduced from 4.2 per cent to 1.2 per cent.[42] The reduction reflected the earlier incidence of costs, a peak GDP decline around 2005, and a partial recovery by 2010.

Another look at the costs of CO_2 regulation was undertaken by the EIA in 2000/01 as part of a cost study of the effects of multi-pollutant legislation being considered by Congress. In line with its earlier work, the effect of NO_X and SO_2 reductions was found to be small compared with implementing a CO_2 cap. The EIA estimated that by 2010, reducing NO_X and SO_2 emissions by 75 per cent below their 1997 levels would cost $6 billion, while the Kyoto requirement for CO_2 alone would cost $88 billion (all with a 2005 start date). Combining the three reductions would save $9 billion to leave approximately $86 billion. Still, the incremental cost of CO_2 abatement of $80 billion represented over 90 per cent of the

---

41   Ibid., pp. xiii, 5.
42   US Energy Information Administration, *Analysis of the Impacts of an Early Start for Compliance with the Kyoto Protocol*, July 1999, p. 10.

total.[43] What the EIA reconfirmed – and what several years later a major study in *Science* by alarmist-camp scientists documented[44] – is that off-the-shelf technology exists to reduce air pollutants but not carbon dioxide emissions.

The private and public sector studies quoted above have been important in the US debate about climate change policy since 1998. Counter-studies outside the peer-reviewed economics literature were not as rigorous and had relatively less influence.[45]

Realism/optimism

Cost–benefit analysis in theory and practice is not a science but an art, since both benefits and costs, monetary and non-monetary, are subjective, fleeting determinations in the mind of present and

---

43 US Energy Information Administration, *Analysis of Strategies for Reducing Multiple Emissions from Power Plants: Sulfur Dioxide, Nitrogen Oxides, and Carbon Dioxide*, December 2000, p. xviii. Also see US Energy Information Administration, *Reducing Emissions of Sulfur Dioxide, Nitrogen Oxides, and Mercury from Electric Power Plants*, September 2001, pp. 16–20, and Marlo Lewis, '"Multi-Pollutant" Regulation of Carbon Dioxide: Shred Politics, Bad Policies', June 2002, available at http://www.cei.org/pdf/3058.pdf.

44 See below, p. 96.

45 One study by Robert Repetto and Duncan Austin ('The Costs of Climate Protection: A Guide for the Perplexed,' World Resources Institute, 1997, p. 8) concluded, 'Under a reasonable standardized set of assumptions, most economic models would predict that the macroeconomic impacts of a carbon tax designed to stabilize carbon emissions would be small and potentially favorable.' The authors' recalculation of benefits and costs assumes, among other things, full international trading, near-competitive costs of non-carbon energies (effective substitution), revenue recycling by government (tax reductions to offset carbon-related revenues), and large avoided climate damages. For an overview of model differences and related issues, see Robert Stavins, 'Economic Analysis of Global Climate Change Policy: A Primer', in Eileen Claussen (ed.), *Climate Change: Science, Strategy, & Solutions*, op. cit., pp. 177–92; and John Weyant, 'Economic Models: How They Work & Why Their Results Differ', in *idem*, pp. 193–208.

future economic actors that are not observable to the outside analyst. Subjective value is not quantifiable since no measure of value (or what economists playfully call 'utils') exists.[46] Nonetheless, potential 'commons problems', which give rise to externalities that cannot be internalised by recognising property rights, invite the best estimate of benefits (avoided damages) and costs (opportunity costs), which must then be compared by discounting future values to the present.

Top-down cost–benefit analysis that is aggregated for simplification is particularly problematic since uncertain climate science is compounded by crude holistic measures of human welfare. Since all climate change is local, cost–benefit calculations should be also. Yet as discussed above, local (regional) analysis of anthropogenic climate change is beyond the pale of climatology and may be for a very long time to come.[47]

Top-down 'integrated assessment' modelling presents a wide range of quantitative estimates that are very uncertain – but better than nothing.[48] Perhaps qualitative direction is all that should be

---

46 A strict interpretation of subjective value denies the appropriateness of cost–benefit analysis for public policy decision-making, preferring instead to recommend private property and other market institutions to promote economic efficiency. See, for example, Roy Cordato, *Welfare Economics and Externalities in an Open Ended Universe*, Kluwer Academic Publishing, Boston, MA, 1992, and *idem*, 'Global Warming, Kyoto, and Tradeable Emissions Permits: The Myth of Efficient Central Planning', Institute for Research on the Economics of Taxation, 1999. Stephen Littlechild has written: 'The task is not primarily one of computing the optimal solution to a well-defined "problem," but rather one of discovering the "problem" in the first place (and the possibility of making some improvement), then gathering and utilizing the necessary information, and finally implementing an improved solution.' Littlechild, *The Fallacy of the Mixed Economy*, Cato Institute, San Francisco, CA, 1979, p. 61.

47 See below, pp. 169–70.

48 The IPCC stated back in 1995: 'The aggregate estimates are subject to considerable uncertainty, but the range of uncertainty cannot be gauged from the

gleaned from them. A *bottom-up* approach that is closer to the economic action, while painstaking and still inexact, is preferable to top-down econometrics. In the climate change debate, the former made a grand entrance in 1999 with *The Impact of Climate Change on the United States Economy*,[49] an anthology of essays assessing benefits and costs given the IPCC base-case estimates of climate change. Economic specialists in such areas as recreation, ecology, natural resources, water and agriculture integrated scientific assumptions such as the CO_2 fertilisation effect and seasonal and diurnal patterns of anthropogenic warming.

Their bottom-up result found that significant climate benefits to offset most or all of the predicted damages in the USA. The book's editors, Robert Mendelsohn and James Neumann, concluded:

> [Climate change] damages in the US [from earlier studies] were estimated to be between 1 and 2 per cent of US GDP. … [Our] new models and methods predict that mild warming will result in a net benefit rather than a net loss to the economy. The likely warming over the next century is expected to make the US economy better off on average.[50]

The Mendelsohn and Neumann study found that net benefit would accrue to the USA given an IPCC-predicted warming of 2.5°C

---

literature. The range of estimates cannot be interpreted as a confidence interval, given the widely differing assumptions and methodologies in the studies.' IPCC, *Economic and Social Dimensions: 1995*, p. 10.

49 Robert Mendelsohn and James Neumann (eds), *The Impact of Climate Change on the United States Economy*, Cambridge University Press, Cambridge, 1999.

50 Robert Mendelsohn and James Neumann, 'Synthesis and Conclusions', in Mendelsohn and Neumann, op. cit. These findings were reconfirmed in Mendelsohn's more recent edited volume, *Global Warming and the American Economy*, Edward Elgar, Northampton, MA, 2001, p. 189.

(4.5°F).[51] Part of this finding resulted from 'agronomic studies suggest[ing] that carbon fertilization is likely to offset some if not all of the damages from warming'.[52] Another driver of this result was the conclusion that 'efficient private adaptation is likely to occur, even if there is no official (government) response to global warming.'[53]

Mendelsohn analysed global costs and benefits from anthropogenic warming in a study for the American Enterprise Institute, *The Greening of Global Warming*. 'The range of predicted effects', he concluded, 'has clearly shifted from being strictly harmful to being ambiguous.'[54] His global conclusion, like his conclusion for the USA, did not assume any increase in weather extremes or negative surprises but was based on the straight warming/precipitation/sea level base case of the IPCC.[55] These findings reinforced the conclusion of an earlier book by economist Thomas Gale Moore that 'most people in most places will be better off in a warmer world'.[56]

While anthropogenic climate change is unlikely to impose substantial cost, its effects will not be uniform in different areas of the world. Mendelsohn calculated that developed countries were net winners (or at least not losers) from expected climate change in the next half-century, but developing counties were net losers owing to their limited ability to adapt to change (whether natural

---

51 Robert Mendelsohn and James Neumann, 'Synthesis and Conclusions', in Mendelsohn and Neumann, op. cit., p. 323.

52 Ibid., p. 321.

53 Robert Mendelsohn and James Neumann, 'Introduction', in Mendelsohn and Neumann, op. cit., p. 5.

54 Robert Mendelsohn, *The Greening of Global Warming*, American Enterprise Institute, Washington, DC, 1999, p. 24.

55 Ibid., pp. 25–26.

56 Thomas Gale Moore, *Climate of Fear: Why We Shouldn't Worry about Global Warming*, Cato Institute, Washington, DC, 1998, p. 157.

or anthropogenic). To address this inequality, Mendelsohn advocates wealth transfers from the winning to losing countries in place of 'expensive short-run abatement programmes' that would have a very small global climate effect.[57]

Open-ended and possibly large wealth transfers are not the only solution. Policy reforms that allow and promote greater geographical mobility within countries and particularly from climate-vulnerable countries are an alternative to Mendelsohn's proposal for wealth redistribution via a Global Environmental Fund. Statist economies need to institute bottom-up property privatisation and establish free-market institutions. Poor countries must reform to allow their inhabitants to become wealthier to better adapt to change and better manage risk.[58]

Favourable economic verdicts from the human influence on climate are not surprising given the present state of knowledge. Climate facts – two centuries into the carbon energy age – do not support model-predicted rapid anthropogenic forcing, an increase in weather extremes and negative surprises. Meanwhile, weather/climate conditions, to whatever extent they are anthropogenic and negative, are being 'internalised' by day-to-day and year-to-year adaptation.[59]

Realism/restraint

Like climate science itself, the popular tool of economic cost–

---

57 Mendelsohn, *The Greening of Global Warming*, op. cit., pp. 27, 30–31.
58 See, generally, Hernando de Soto, *The Mystery of Capital*, Basic Books, New York, 2002.
59 Adaptation can range from greater investments in indoor air conditioning and outdoor mist machines to greater geographical mobility where individuals and groups migrate to preferred climates seasonally or permanently.

benefit analysis crucially depends on realism to reach the most informed conclusions. Yet it must cope with a high order of complexity and inherent uncertainty as a forecasting tool. The initial task for the economic prognosticator is to determine whether the predicted effects of the proposed policy are desirable or undesirable – by no means a trivial task.

Two perennial issues in cost–benefit analysis are magnified in the special case of climate-change policy. First, the standard procedure is to discount future benefits and costs to the present time for comparison. The impact of discounting is dominant when one considers that current expenditures may not reveal benefits for decades. Second, cost–benefit analysis has an inherent bias in favour of a 'planned' solution. Government intervention is designed to solve a perceived problem; what cannot easily be perceived is all the ways in which the 'solution' will turn out to be problematic. The discounting and politicisation problems are discussed below.

Discounting

A universal law of economics is *time preference*. That is, individuals place a higher value on a satisfaction unit of income received now than in the future, other things being equal. A positive rate of interest for discounting accounts for pure time preference and, if that interest rate is 'risk adjusted', also accounts for any uncertainty surrounding future outcomes.[60]

Discounting of long-term future benefits is a barrier for

---

60 Ludwig von Mises, *Human Action*, Contemporary Books, Chicago, IL, 1966, pp. 483–90. For a popular economics textbook discussion of interest rates and discounting, see Roy Ruffin and Paul Gregory, *Principles of Economics*, Addison Wesley, New York, 2001, pp. 330–36.

Figure 11 **Discounted future benefits**

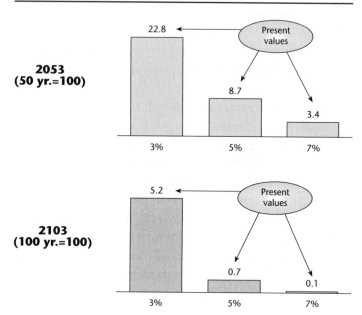

Note: The discounting formula to calculate net present values for a future assumed value is PV = FV/(1+r)^n where PV is present value, FV is future value, r is the interest rate used for discounting, and n the number of years.

proponents of immediate policy action in terms of addressing distant possible problems. Near-term costs carry more weight than long-term benefits in economic terms. For example, a discount rate of 5 per cent means that one pound of benefit 50 years from now (2053) is worth only eight to nine pence today. One pound of benefit in one hundred years is worth less than one penny today. The changing time value of money for different interest rates is illustrated in Figure 11.

Proponents of GHG restrictions whose strategies are economically sub-optimal in a discounting framework have attempted to overcome this problem by changing the parameters of the analysis. They describe long-term projects as effectively 'inter-generational' transactions; therefore the 'proper' discount rate should be low or zero on equity or moral grounds.[61] Yet the inter-generational equity argument is contradicted by the fact that in a world of positive social and economic trends,[62] future society will be more technologically and materially able to capitalise on positive climate change and ameliorate negative climate change. This discounting, assuming general progress, not only has an *economic* basis but also a *fairness* dimension. Why disadvantage individuals now to help better-situated individuals decades (or centuries) from now? And in purely economic terms, why not turn (forgone) costs into immediate benefits that can be compounded over time? It is difficult to imagine that future generations would want us to substitute low-return investments for those that would have earned higher returns and then wish to put themselves in the same predicament.

This point can be illustrated by an example. Assume that a reasonable risk-adjusted discount rate that could be used to assess action to improve environmental conditions is 5 per cent per year.[63] Assume also that £100 million is to be invested today to achieve

61 For a challenge to traditional discounting principles to justify increased intergenerational environmental wealth transfers, see Paul Portney and John Weyant (eds), *Discounting and Intergenerational Equity*, Resources for the Future, Washington, DC, 1999. A criticism of the 'moral' or 'prescriptive' approach to discounting is made by Brian Mannix, 'How Much Do We Care about the Deep Future?', *Regulation* 23(2), 2000, pp. 55–57.

62 See the books referenced on p. 23, footnote 1.

63 Five per cent compares with risk-free real rates of returns from long-term, index-linked government bonds, which have tended to vary between just under 2.5 per cent and 4 per cent, and there should also be a considerable risk premium incorporated in any discount rate used to assess the benefits of current expenditure to bring about imprecise future environmental benefits.

£150 million of environmental benefits in 40 years' time. Market interest rates indicate the time preference that individuals have for consumption now but also indicate the rate of return on alternative projects. Thus the £100 million could be invested at 5 per cent to produce £704 million in 40 years' time (i.e. £100$(1.05)^{40}$ million). To spend £100 million to obtain £150 million of benefits has an opportunity cost of £704 million of benefits that could have been obtained at the same time by investing in an alternative project.

Discounting is an economically rational way of ensuring that the opportunity cost of environmental action is taken into account: it cannot be assumed away by changing the paradigm. Otherwise, the debate degenerates from rational and realistic to emotive.

Politicisation versus optimisation

A major omission of cost–benefit analysis is a reduction of benefits and/or increase in costs to account for *politicisation* – the reality that any 'optimal' policy designed by social scientists will be likely to move in 'non-optimal' directions before or after finalisation and implementation.[64] A leading economics textbook has put government failure on the same plane as market failure:

> Economists are not starry-eyed about the government
> any more than they are about the market. Governments
> can make bad decisions or carry out good ideas badly.

---

64   'This is not to suggest that political pressures are undesirable, or that governments should not respond to them. The argument is, rather, that governments inevitably *will* respond to political pressures. It cannot be assumed that the use of cost–benefit analysis and externality taxes will ensure the remedy of externalities in the manner assumed by many welfare economists.' Littlechild, op. cit., p. 62.

> Indeed, just as there are market failures such as monopoly and pollution, so are there 'government failures' in which government interventions lead to waste or redistribute income in an undesirable fashion.[65]

The unanticipated or even intended twists and turns could reflect the will of a political majority or special interests in a democratic setting or the brute edict of an authoritarian regime. A politicisation risk factor should be estimated for real-world guidance, but mainstream modelling has been slow to incorporate this reality owing to estimation difficulties. Nothing is judged better than something, quite unlike in virtually every other area of climate modelling.

The risk of implementing the Kyoto Protocol or any other multinational or international programme to govern the carbon cycle is that newly created institutions will take on a life of their own. Sub-optimal policies, not a 'Pareto optimal' policy, will result. Thus any cost–benefit model must factor in politicisation costs and risks before advocating policy activism beyond 'no regrets'. In this way, government failure can be evaluated along with the alleged market failure.

One relevant analogy for the climate policy debate from the energy field concerns the US Mandatory Oil Import Program (MOIP), a federal programme that set maximum quotas on the amount of oil that was imported into America from 1959 to 1972. The programme was initially voluntary but after two years became mandatory with a singular focus on promoting 'national security'

---

65 Paul Samuelson and William Nordhaus, *Economics*, Irwin McGraw-Hill, New York, 1998, pp. 287–88.

by protecting domestic oil producers. The programme became distorted over time as political forces allocated oil import rights on a variety of grounds – welfare, equity, environmental and macroeconomic – that were inconsistent with the original aims of the programme.[66] There are many other examples in the energy and non-energy fields of programmes that violated their original premises along the way.

Sequestration versus mitigation

A major study published in *Science* by eighteen authors forth-rightly concluded that the technology does not exist to shift from carbon energies to low-carbon ones. The mass quantities are not available, and what supply there could be cannot be produced at an acceptable cost to society. 'Revolutionary changes in the technology of energy production, distribution, storage, and conversion' are required, changes that 'cannot be simply regulated' into being.[67] Among the options the study examined was sequestration, an 'enormous' undertaking that would require 'substantial research investments'.[68]

A more recent study in *Science* concluded that carbon sequestration is a more viable alternative than carbon mitigation to balance the carbon cycle in the short to medium term, if not longer. The author concluded that very large quantities of carbon could be captured at a future cost of around $30 per ton, or about $13

---

66 See, generally, Douglas Bohi and Milton Russell, *Limiting Oil Imports: An Economic History and Analysis*, Johns Hopkins University Press, Baltimore, MD, 1978.

67 Hoffert et al., op. cit., pp. 981, 986.

68 Ibid., p. 983.

per barrel for oil. The author concluded: 'Today's urgent need for substantive CO_2 emission reductions could be satisfied more cheaply by available sequestration technology than by an immediate transition to nuclear, wind or solar energy. Further development of sequestration would assure plentiful, low-cost energy for the century, giving better alternatives ample time to mature.'[69]

Conclusion

Climate economics has many uncertainties because it begins with climatology and biogeochemistry unknowns and introduces its own uncertainties. But the positive effect of CO_2 fertilisation, the benign distribution of anthropogenic warming and the balance of evidence towards lower warming and precipitation scenarios lead to a conclusion that there will be important economic benefits to offset anticipated and unanticipated climate-change costs. The discounting of future benefits to the present time for comparison with the costs of mandatory carbon constraint has profound implications for the conclusions of economic cost–benefit analysis – and for the policy side of the climate debate. Similarly the introduction of the concept of 'government failure' into models significantly reduces the attractiveness of policy activism.

How can climate models be compared with integrated assessment economic models? Both are 'mainstream' exercises, so it would be inconsistent for a policy-maker to reject one and not the other. One could reject *both* on the grounds that drawing conclusions from imperfect models is not 'better than nothing', but then the perfect might become the enemy of the good. In the field of

69   Klaus Lackner, 'A Guide to CO_2 Sequestration', *Science*, 13 June 2003, p. 1,678.

climate modelling across the disciplines, a frequent result is that climate alarmism from climate models is joined by economic 'alarmism' from top-down economic modelling.

Some middle ground can be proposed, however. Climate modelling in its current state can be largely, if not wholly, demoted because of its inherent high-warming feedback bias, discussed above. Top-down economic modelling can be demoted because of its potential bias against innovation, since by definition the new is not known in the present. This leaves bottom-up cost–benefit analysis as the most technically insightful method to translate science into economics for public policy decision-making, which makes the (non-alarmist) studies by Robert Mendelsohn et al. particularly important.

5 FRAMING THE POLICY ISSUES

A proper economic analysis of climate change mitigates the alarm and casts doubt on the case for policy activism. A paradigm that competes against climate economics is that of *climate stasism* coupled with a particular interpretation of the precautionary principle. This view supports ambitious government activism to restructure the energy economy and control land usage to balance the carbon cycle. In the extreme, such climate planning tends towards world economic/environmental planning, or what Al Gore called the 'central organizing principle for civilization',[1] albeit with taxation and 'market mechanisms' such as emissions trading instead of government ownership of the means of production or highly prescriptive command-and-control regulation. But effective control in this approach must be globally coordinated. This energy-sustainability programme can be sharply contrasted with the here-and-now, objective energy sustainability problem – poverty bred by statist policies that sabotage the free-market improvement process.

---

1   'We must make the rescue of the environment the central organizing principle for civilization. Whether we realize it or not, we are now engaged in an epic battle to right the balance of our earth, and the tide of this battle will turn only when the majority of people in the world become sufficiently aroused by a shared sense of urgent danger to join an all-out effort.' Al Gore, *Earth in the Balance: Ecology and the Human Spirit*, Plume/Penguin, New York, 1992, 1993, p. 269.

The Kyoto conundrum

The Kyoto Protocol is at the global centre of policy activism regarding anthropogenic climate change. It is an agreement that then US Vice-President Al Gore rescued from collapse at the eleventh hour back in 1997 by ignoring the unanimous advice from the US Senate not to enter into an agreement that did not include developing countries or that was detrimental to the US economy.[2] Approximately 38 Annex 1 countries, representing the developed world, agreed to reduce their emissions to 5.2 per cent below 1990 levels by 2008–12.[3] Nations from the developing world, accounting for over one third of global emissions, were exempted from mandatory reductions, and these countries – including China, India and Mexico – went further to block any language about voluntary reductions.

The protocol is seen by its adherents as the beginning phase of a long international march towards the stabilisation of atmospheric greenhouse gases at roughly double their pre-industrial level (about 550 ppmv). More realistically, however, Kyoto represents both a beginning and an end, since compliance in the 2008–12 compliance period – and more so after this period – is unrealistic. In the words of one study: 'Paradoxically, Kyoto is too weak and too strong: Too strong because its initial cuts are perceived as an economic burden by some (the United States withdrew for this stated reason); too weak because much greater emission reductions will be needed and we lack the technology to make them.'[4]

---

2   William Stevens, *The Change in the Weather*, Dell Publishing, New York, 1999, pp. 305–6.

3   Michael Grubb et al., *The Kyoto Protocol: A Guide and Assessment*, Royal Institute of International Affairs, London, 1999, pp. 115–19, 301.

4   Hoffert et al., op. cit., p. 981.

Figure 12 **World CO$_2$ emissions**
  Million tonnes

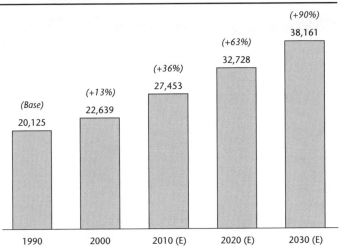

E = estimated
Note: International Energy Agency carbon estimates refer to carbon dioxide and not the carbon equivalent of other greenhouse gases (ibid., p. 80).
Source: International Energy Agency, *World Energy Outlook 2002*, IEA/OECD, Paris, 2002, p. 413.

The International Energy Agency (IEA), affiliated with the 30-member countries of the Organisation for Economic Cooperation and Development (OECD), forecasts that global carbon dioxide emissions in the next few decades will rise at a slightly higher pace than overall energy demand – 1.8 per cent per year. As can be seen in Figure 12, the overall forecast increase by 2030, the last year of the forecast, is 90 per cent above 1990 levels (and 70 per cent above 2000 levels).

The IEA's forecast for OECD Europe is that carbon emissions will be 10 per cent higher than 1990 levels by 2010 and 18 per cent greater by 2020 – a major business-as-usual challenge for Kyoto's

Figure 13   **CO₂ emissions: OECD Europe versus US/Canada**
Million tonnes

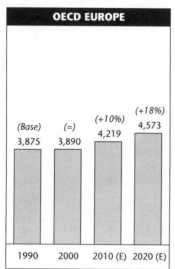
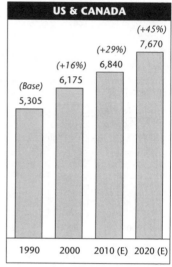

Note: International Energy Agency carbon estimates refer to carbon dioxide and not the carbon equivalent of other greenhouse gases (ibid., p. 80). OECD European countries are Austria, Belgium, the Czech Republic, Denmark, Finland, France, Germany, Greece, Hungary, Iceland, Ireland, Italy, Luxembourg, the Netherlands, Norway, Poland, Portugal, Spain, Sweden, Switzerland, Turkey, and the United Kingdom. (Non-European Union members are in bold.)
Source: International Energy Agency, *World Energy Outlook 2002*, IEA/OECD, Paris, 2002, pp. 425, 433.

requirements.[5] Still, this estimate is much lower than that projected for the USA and Canada on the one hand and OECD Europe on the other hand, as seen in Figure 13.[6]

The disparity between Europe and the USA explains their very different views about the fairness of the Kyoto Protocol and its effects on their economies. President Bush stated the obvious:

5   International Energy Agency, *World Energy Outlook 2002*, op. cit., p. 417.
6   Ibid., pp. 425, 433.

'Kyoto is, in many ways, unrealistic. Many countries cannot meet their Kyoto targets; the targets themselves were arbitrary and not based upon science. For America, complying with those mandates would have a negative economic impact, with layoffs of workers and price increases for consumers.'[7]

What President Bush should have added is that the decision of Europe to pursue carbon cutbacks beyond free-market no-regrets policy (defined in Chapter 6), even if those were smaller than those assigned to the USA, is bad for America since the world economy would become poorer. *Globalisation makes the Kyoto Protocol everyone's problem.*

A huge compliance gulf exists between Europe and the developing world. Figure 14 compares OECD Europe emissions with developing country emissions as forecast by the IEA for 2010, 2020 and 2030.[8] While both regions had about the same relative emissions in 1990, CO_2 emissions in the developing world have surged ahead of OECD Europe since. The IEA forecasts that developing-world emissions will be more than triple those of OECD Europe by 2020. This explains why non-Annex 1 countries refused to agree to mandatory or voluntary emission reduction targets in the Kyoto Protocol.

Compliance with the Kyoto Protocol is virtually impossible for its signatories as a whole nearly six years into the agreement. Yet perfect compliance is no panacea from the viewpoint of climate alarmists. Noted climatologist Tom Wigley summarised the Kyoto climate scenarios as follows:

> Three scenarios for post-Kyoto emissions reductions [indicate that] ... the long-term [temperature]

---

7   George W. Bush, 'President's Address on Global Climate Change', White House News Release, Office of Press Secretary, 11 June 2001.

8   International Energy Agency, *World Energy Outlook 2002*, op. cit., p. 461.

Figure 14 **CO₂ emissions: OECD Europe versus developing countries**
Million tonnes

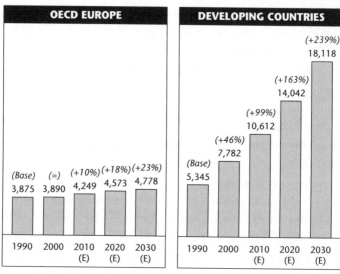

Source: International Energy Agency, *World Energy Outlook 2002*, IEA/OECD, Paris, 2002, pp. 433, 461.

consequences are small. ... The influence of the Protocol
[to reduce anthropogenic warming] would, furthermore,
be undetectable for many decades. ... The prospects for
stabilizing sea level over coming centuries are remote, so it
is not surprising that the Protocol has such minor effects.[9]

Wigley's study of the climate effects of Kyoto compliance
shows that only about 5 per cent of the human influence on
climate would be reversed if the Kyoto commitments remained

9   Tom M. L. Wigley, 'The Kyoto Protocol: CO_2, CH_4 and Climate Implications',
     Geophysical Research Letters, 1 July 1998, pp. 2,285, 2,288.

Figure 15 **Kyoto temperature effect: year 2100**

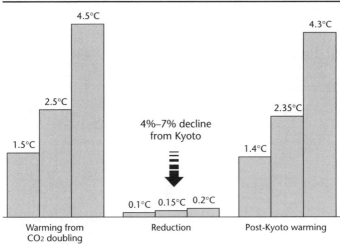

Source: Tom M. L. Wigley, 'The Kyoto Protocol: CO_2, CH_4 and Climate Implications', *Geophysical Research Letters*, 1 July 1998, pp. 2,285, 2,288.

honoured from the first compliance period (2008–12) through to the end of the century, as seen in Figures 15 and 16.

Alarmists cite this evidence to warn that much more policy activism and energy restructuring will be needed in the future to control anthropogenic warming. It is estimated that a 60–80 per cent reduction in worldwide CO_2 emissions will be necessary to stabilise atmospheric concentrations at 1990 levels, compared with a 5.2 per cent reduction from 1990 levels – for developed countries only – in the Kyoto Protocol.[10] Prominent scientists have

10 Statement of Robert Watson in *The Kyoto Protocol: The Undermining of American Prosperity – the Science*, Hearing before the Committee on Small Business, House of Representatives, 105th Congress, Second Session, Government Printing Office, Washington, DC, 1998, p. 5.

Figure 16 **Kyoto sea-level effect: year 2100**
Centimetres

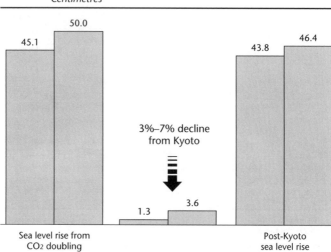

Source: Tom M. L. Wigley, 'The Kyoto Protocol: CO_2, CH_4 and Climate Implications', *Geophysical Research Letters*, 1 July 1998, pp. 2,285, 2,288.

estimated the number of Kyotos that will be needed at between ten and thirty.[11] Given the inevitable implementation deficiencies, the top end of the number of necessary agreements would increase.

The Kyoto Protocol is a climatic non-event, leaving its sponsors with symbolism in the short run and the need for many further wrenching agreements over the medium to long term. As time erodes the current agreement, a substitute international agreement will be sought. But the same inherent problems will re-emerge as regards winners and losers,[12] the lack of an international

11 Bradley, *Julian Simon*, op. cit., p. 117.
12 'The difficulty of achieving a global agreement on climate change [involves] … the heterogeneity of countries with respect to the causes of climate change, the

enforcement mechanism,[13] subjective valuations of sinks versus sources, and energy, economic and political realities. This is why a group of scientists from the climate alarmism camp, including Tom Wigley, gave a back-door slap to Kyoto by concluding that 'the fossil fuel greenhouse effect is an energy problem that cannot be simply regulated away'.[14]

Stasism and 'problematic' warming

Climate alarmism and its corollary, policy activism, rest on several interrelated arguments and assertions, including:

- The growing imbalance of the carbon cycle cannot be good for a fragile climate.
- Climate models showing high climate sensitivity to GHG build-up are to be accepted at face value.

---

impacts, and the mitigation and adaptation costs. ... The strong incentives to free-ride on the global agreement and the lack of related sanctions. ... The absence of environmental leadership ... [and] the focus on a single international climate agreement.' Intergovernmental Panel on Climate Change, *Climate Change 2001: Mitigation*, Cambridge University Press, Cambridge, 2001, p. 627.

13   'The general nature of the commitments contained in the [Climate] Convention would, in any case, prove difficult to enforce. These factors explain why parties have not endowed the supreme body of the Convention, the [Conference of Parties], with the authority to impose legally binding consequences on a Party in the event of non-compliance. Thus at present, no legal body exists to enforce compliance in the climate change context.' Ibid., p. 432. Furthermore (ibid., p. 627), 'When all countries agree to control emissions, a defecting country achieves the whole benefit, because its incidence of global emission is marginal (with a few exceptions) and pays no cost. Hence a defection with respect to a large coalition is the optimal strategy if there are no sanctions. However, credible sanctions are difficult to design. Emissions themselves are hardly a credible sanction, because countries are unlikely to sustain self-damaging policies.'

14   Hoffert et al., op. cit., pp. 983–85.

- A 'greenhouse signal' with increasing weather extremes will be likely to appear if it has not already.
- Surprises cannot be positive but only negative.
- Precaution is called for given that 'small changes in the mean climate or climate variability can produce relatively large changes in the frequency of extreme events (defined as events where a certain threshold is passed); a small change in the variability has a stronger effect than a similar change in the mean'.[15]
- Humankind has unwittingly created 'the planetary gamble that we cannot afford to lose'[16] given today's atmospheric GHG concentrations which are at their highest level in hundreds of thousands of years, and today's warming which could be the highest in a thousand years.

Thus some have called for a 'prudent' public policy standard of judging the anthropogenic influence guilty until proven innocent.[17] Consequently, a policy recommendation has emerged from this camp to cap atmospheric concentrations of greenhouse gases to a carbon-equivalent level of 550 ppmv by 2050, roughly twice the pre-industrial level.[18] Such a course would mean, in the words

---

15   IPCC, *Climate Change 1995: the Science*, p. 290. Also see ibid., p. 336.

16   This is the subtitle to Stephen Schneider's 1997 book *Laboratory Earth: The Planetary Gamble that We Can't Afford to Lose*, Basic Books, New York, 1997.

17   Tom Wigley et al., 'Indices and Indicators of Climate Change: Issues of Detection, Validation and Climate Sensitivity', in Irving Mintzer (ed.), *Confronting Climate Change: Risks, Implications and Responses*, Cambridge University Press, Cambridge, 1992, p. 87.

18   Royal Commission on Environmental Pollution, *Energy – the Changing Climate*, RCEP, London, 2000, p. 2.

of Paul Ehrlich, 'that the era of fossil-fuel dominance must soon be brought to an end'.[19]

Climate alarmists gloss over the benefits of anthropogenic climate change. In their view, the human influence cannot be good – only bad. Otherwise, they would have to concede the possibility that some level of anthropogenic warming was good, a higher level neutral, and a still higher level preferable to costly public policies to address the issue. Many alarmists avoid arguments over what these warming levels might be since such a debate would detract from the urgency of solving the problem that has been pre-determined to exist.

The philosophy behind climate alarmism is *stasism*, which sees 'a good future [as] either the product of detailed, technocratic blueprints or the return to an idealized stable past'.[20] The *dynamist* view, in contrast, welcomes change in the belief that benefits accrue in 'a world of constant creation, discovery, and competition'.[21]

Climate stasism avoids the debate that is necessary in a world of scarce means to achieve competing and unlimited ends. The key question for the debate is what level of anthropogenic warming is potentially problematic? The aforementioned collaborative work by leading climate economists taking a bottom-up modelling approach found net benefits for the USA and a split between regional winners and losers globally from a 2.5°C (4.5°F) warming.[22] An estimate of problematic warming by Stephen Schneider, a climate

19 Paul and Anne Ehrlich, *Healing the Planet*, Addison-Wesley, New York, 1991, p. 45. A later proposal to phase out fossil fuels over ten years has been put forward by Ross Gelbspan in his book *The Heat Is On*, Addison-Wesley, New York, 1997, p. 187.

20 Virginia Postrel, *The Future and Its Enemies*, Free Press, New York, 1998, p. xii.

21 Ibid., p. xiv.

22 See pp. 88–9.

scientist whose writings have put him in the alarmist camp, is 3.5°C (6.3°F).[23] A World Energy Council report concluded, 'Although some research suggests that the potential for adaptation of food supply to climate change is substantial, significant increases in global crop yields or of specific crops which may occur from a 2°C warming are liable to turn to a loss for a 4°C warming.'[24] A more alarmist interpretation by two scientists estimates that anthropogenic warming of 1°C will lead to coral bleaching, 2°C will lead to the diminution of the West Antarctic Ice Sheet, and 3°C to a shutdown of the ocean's thermohaline circulation system.[25] The latter problem, it is believed, could trigger a new ice age for Europe.

These scenarios and estimates are, however, very uncertain, and they are still only part of a much larger picture that would include potential long-term positive effects of anthropogenic climate change such as preventing a return of a little ice age – or even supporting the thermohaline circulation system. And even then, economic factors should be included along with ecological ones in the calculus of danger.

A 'safe' level of GHG concentrations in the atmosphere for long-term guidance has not been scientifically determined.[26]

---

23 Stephen Schneider, 'What Is "Dangerous" Climate Change?', op. cit., pp. 17–19. Schneider's worry with anthropogenic warming is evident in two of his books: *Global Warming: Are We Entering the Greenhouse Century?*, Sierra Club Books, San Francisco, CA, 1989, and *Laboratory Earth: The Planetary Gamble that We Can't Afford to Lose*, op. cit.

24 J. M. Jefferson, 'Post-Rio '92 – Developments Relating to Climate Change', World Energy Council, Report No. 2, March 1995, p. 8.

25 Brian O'Neill and Michael Oppenheimer, 'Dangerous Climate Impacts and the Kyoto Protocol', *Science*, 14 June 2002, pp. 1,971–72.

26 National Research Council, *Climate Change Science: An Analysis of Some Key Questions*, NRC, Washington, DC, 2001, p. 4.

Given an anthropogenic warming forecast of 0.15°C (+/−0.05°C) per decade 'over the next several decades' by James Hansen and Makiko Sato,[27] and a similar estimate by other mainstream climate modellers,[28] a forecast that is at the top of the range estimated by Hansen's opponent Patrick Michaels a decade ago,[29] an alarmist policy response is not self-evidently appropriate. Substantial uncertainties remain, which brings us to an analysis of the *precautionary principle* for policy guidance.

The precautionary principle

The precautionary principle is an important policy argument in the climate change debate. The United Nations Framework Convention on Climate Change (1992) stated, 'Where there are threats of serious or irreversible damage, lack of full scientific certainty shall not be used as a reason for postponing cost-effective measures to prevent environmental degradation.'[30] The World Energy Council, attempting to balance the need to alleviate energy poverty with policies addressing climate change, has advocated a 'minimum regret' public policy criterion, including 'a broader agenda to achieve urgent and effective action'.[31] Lord Browne, the

27 James Hansen and Makiko Sato, 'Trends of Measured Climate Forcing Agents', *Proceedings of the National Academy of Sciences*, 18 December 2001, pp. 14,778–83.

28 Myles Allen et al., 'Quantifying the Uncertainty in Forecasts of Anthropogenic Climate Change', *Nature*, 5 October 2000, pp. 617–20.

29 Patrick Michaels, *Sound and Fury: The Science and Politics of Global Warming*, Cato Institute, Washington, DC, 1992, p. 187. Michaels provided a best guess of doubled GHG concentrations of 1.4°C in his second book (Patrick Michaels and Robert Balling, *The Satanic Gases: Clearing the Air on Global Warming*, Cato Institute, Washington, DC, 2000, p. 56).

30 See the discussion in Grubb et al., op. cit., p. 38.

31 World Energy Council, 'Potential Climate Change', Report No. 4, September 1995, p. 21.

head of bp, has established new profit centres around carbon reduction in the name of the precautionary principle.[32]

Policy activism to mitigate GHG emissions reflects a one-sided application of the precautionary principle, by focusing only on the acts of man on the natural environment and not on the acts of public policy on the economy. As one scholar has noted:

> The fatal flaw in the precautionary case for Kyoto – as in environmental advocacy generally – is its complete one-sidedness. Environmentalists demand assurances of no harm only with respect to actions that government might regulate, never with respect to government regulation itself. But government intervention frequently boomerangs, creating the very risks that precautionists deem intolerable. … So here is a precautionary argument *against* the Kyoto Protocol. … Until the Kyoto Protocol is proved to be safe, we should oppose it.[33]

Making energy more expensive or less reliable through the implementation of the precautionary principle has political limits in the developed world and creates a dilemma regarding the estimated 1.6 billion people currently living in energy poverty.[34] The precautionary principle can be seen as elitist and a 'regressive' tax on poorer countries. One economist explained:

> Politically, the precautionary principle is offered as a radical,

---

32 See, for example, Janet Guyon, 'A Big-Oil Man Gets Religion', *Fortune*, 6 March 2000, pp. 87–89. bp's strategy includes investments in solar and emissions trading and a public relations effort to differentiate itself from rival Exxon Mobil, particularly in Europe, where climate alarmism has reached an almost religious fervour.

33 Marlo Lewis, 'Why Kyoto Is Not an Insurance Policy', in *The Kyoto Protocol*, op. cit., pp. 79–80.

34 International Energy Agency, *World Energy Outlook 2002*, op. cit., p. 365.

even revolutionary, doctrine when in reality it is way beyond conservative in being fundamentally reactionary and elitist. More than even the most conservative doctrines, it assumes that the status quo is privileged and free of danger. This may be fine today for comfortable elites, but it adversely impacts the disadvantaged, particularly those in poorer countries who need technological change to raise their living standards and improve their lives.[35]

Policy activism based on the precautionary principle carries a magnified risk of economic error since the potential problem is large and undefined enough to inspire a central planning approach. One economist noted:

> Using the precautionary principle therefore means dwelling on problems with no current solutions – or, more precisely, in a curious reversion to early postwar thinking, assuming that the only ways around the massive future problems which appear to exist are through central planning. A society dedicated to use of the precautionary principle would seem likely, over the years, to generate excessive regulation and indeed eventually to revert to much of the apparatus of central control which used to exist before the revival of economic liberalism.[36]

The precautionary principle applies not only to climate change but also to climate-change policy, since both involve human welfare. Policy advice given a decade ago by the US National Academy of Sciences, National Academy of Engineering and Institute of

35 Thomas DeGregori, *Agriculture and Modern Technology: A Defense*, Iowa State University Press, Ames, IA, 2001, pp. 121–22.

36 Colin Robinson, 'Energy Economists and Economic Liberalism', *Energy Journal* 21(2), 2000, p. 20.

Figure 17 **Global energy poverty**

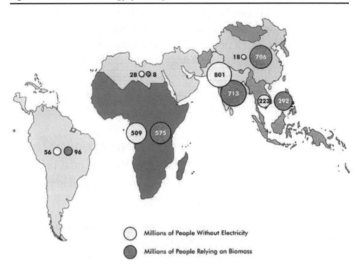

Source: Reprinted from International Energy Agency, *World Energy Outlook 2002*, IEA/OECD, Paris, 2002, p. 372.

Medicine on the climate-change issue still applies today: 'Errors of doing too much can be as consequential as errors of doing too little; the error of trying to solve the wrong problem is as likely as the error of failing to act.'[37]

Poverty

The major challenge for energy sustainability in the new century is eradicating energy poverty. The World Energy Council and In-

37   National Academy of Sciences et al., *Policy Implications of Greenhouse Warming*, National Academy Press, Washington, DC, 1992, p. 194.

ternational Energy Agency estimate that 1.6 billion people – over one quarter of the global population – still do not have access to electricity and other modern forms of energy.[38] A total of 2.4 billion people rely on wood and dung – primitive biomass – for home cooking and heating. These individuals, concentrated in South Asia and sub-Saharan Africa, as seen in Figure 17, suffer from acute smoke inhalation, subsistence productivity and unsanitary living conditions. A study by the United Nations and the World Energy Council estimated that 2 million premature deaths per year occur from primitive biomass pollution alone.[39]

The benefits of electrification can easily be overlooked by intellectuals, policy-makers and the voting public in the Annex 1 countries, where over 99 per cent of the people use electricity routinely. The International Energy Agency described the upside of greater energy availability for the poor as follows:

> Modern energy services enhance the life of the poor in countless ways. Electric light extends the day, providing extra hours for reading and work. Modern cook-stoves save women and children from daily exposure to noxious cooking fumes. Refrigeration allows local clinics to keep needed medicines on hand. And modern energy can directly reduce poverty by raising a poor country's productivity and extending the quality and range of its products – thereby putting more wages into the pockets of the deprived.[40]

38   World Energy Council, *Energy for Tomorrow's World: Acting Now!*, Atalink Projects, London, 2000, p. 5; International Energy Agency, *World Energy Outlook 2002*, op. cit., p. 26.

39   UNDP, UNDESA and WEC, *World Energy Assessment: Energy and the Challenge of Energy Sustainability*, United Nations Publications, New York, 2000, p. 15.

40   International Energy Agency, *World Energy Outlook 2002*, op. cit., p. 366.

While progress has been made – 27 per cent of the world's population was not connected to electricity supplies in 2000 compared with 51 per cent in 1970 – the International Energy Agency predicts that, 'in the absence of vigorous new policies, 1.4 billion people [17 per cent] will still lack electricity in 2030'.[41]

Regional energy poverty amid global energy plenty is the direct result of economic statism whereby non-existent or poorly enforced property rights hamper market exchange (including regulatory risk for international investment in energy provision), and poor legal institutions have stymied human ingenuity and progress.[42] This is greatly different from the position in market economies where the average person is simultaneously increasing energy usage and reducing pollution.

Damage from climate change is particularly acute for the most vulnerable regions of the world that have the least ability to cope with weather extremes or adapt to new climatic circumstances over the longer term. Poverty magnifies the damage caused by extreme weather events. Thus poverty, not weather or climate change, is the primary sustainability issue, and poverty eradication via sound economic policies is the major policy imperative. If climate-change policies work against policies that would otherwise lead to increased living standards, economic and thus environmental sustainability may worsen in the short run.[43] Thus, 'the moral imperative should be not to prevent human disruption of the environment but to ameliorate the social and political con-

41   Ibid., pp. 365, 373, 377.
42   See de Soto, op. cit; and Guillermo Yeatts, *Subsoil Wealth: The Struggle for Privatization in Argentina*, Foundation for Economic Education, Irvington-on-Hudson, NY, 1997.
43   Lomborg, op. cit., pp. 305–24, 348–52. Also see Goklany, op. cit., pp. 189–213.

ditions that lead people to behave in environmentally disruptive ways'.[44]

The same may be true if climate-change policies reduce energy availability or affordability for populations that are industrialising. Another potentially threatening trade-off between climate policy activism and living standards concerns international trade restrictions (such as sanctions) that pose as enforcement mechanisms for global climate-change regulatory governance.[45] Any of these 'solutions' hampers economic coordination and growth, the very things that foster adaptation to weather and climate change from any cause.

Climate-change policies for the developing world should be designed to pass a short-run poverty eradication test.

- Will the policies make energy expansion more likely?
- Will climate policies make energy more affordable and reliable?
- Will the policies promote the priority of moving statist economies towards sustainability via the institutions of private property, voluntary exchange and the rule of law?

If the answer to any of these questions is 'no', climate-change

---

44 Daniel Sarewitz and Robert Pielke, 'Breaking the Global-Warming Gridlock', *Atlantic Monthly*, July 2000, p. 63.

45 See, generally, Duncan Brack, *International Trade and Climate Change Policies*, Royal Institute of International Affairs, London, 2000. On the clash between national sovereignty and the Kyoto Protocol, see Jeremy Rabkin, *Why Sovereignty Matters*, American Enterprise Institute, Washington, DC, 1998, ch. 7. For the inherent problems of Kyoto's proposed international carbon trading scheme, see David Victor, *The Collapse of the Kyoto Protocol and the Struggle to Slow Global Warming*, Princeton University Press, Princeton, NJ, 2001.

policy is promoting poverty sustainability, not energy sustainability.

For developed countries where poverty is not acute, a health-is-wealth standard should guide public policy. Regulatory programmes intended to promote health, including those perceived to mitigate man-made climate change, must overcome a health penalty that intrinsically occurs when private-sector wealth is lost through taxation or regulatory burdens.[46] This 'opportunity cost' part of the cost–benefit equation is another barrier between scientific indications of a human impact on climate and an activist public policy intended to mitigate climate change.

Conclusion

The economics of climate change sets up the framework for climate policy. Policy guidance is provided by a close examination of the relative burdens of the Kyoto Protocol for the developed and developing worlds, by the hidden assumption about a natural climate optimum (stasism), and by the application of the precautionary principle. This leaves the public policy question, 'What should be done beyond "no regrets", if anything, to address the growing concentration of long-lived greenhouse gases emitted into the atmosphere?'

---

46 See John Graham and Jonathan Wiener (eds), *Risk versus Risk: Tradeoffs in Protecting Health and the Environment*, Harvard University Press, Cambridge, MA, 1995; and Robert Hahn (ed.), *Risk, Costs, and Lives Saved*, Oxford University Press, Washington, DC, 1996.

6   CLIMATE POLICY

Climate policy can range from the purely suggestive and voluntary to voluntary measures combined with government subsidies and persuasion (the policy now developing in the USA) to various mandatory emission reduction strategies (generally the policy of the EU). Given the steep emissions trajectory and the global quest for economic improvement, there is limited room for fundamental emissions cutbacks. The differences in emissions cutbacks proposed by different proponents of carbon suppression would yield, in practice, differences in global warming outcomes of only a few tenths of a degree over a century. The good news is that there does not need to be a fundamental restructuring of the world's energy economy given the increasing sustainability of carbon energies in so many respects.

'No regrets' GHG reductions

Public policy towards the climate-change issue should begin – and can end – with reforms that make sense in their own right; that is, 'win-win' initiatives that reduce emissions but do not hurt energy consumers or taxpayers. These initiatives include:

* Removing subsidies that keep energy prices below market

levels, thereby reducing energy demand and eliminating related emissions.[1]

- Introducing 'peak' (congestion) pricing when demand is highest in transportation and retail gas and electricity markets to reduce demand and eliminate related emissions.[2]

- Reducing emissions of the air pollutants, especially particulate matter (PM_{10}), nitrogen oxides (NO_x) and carbon monoxide (CO), to levels in compliance with the tightening standards of the US Clean Air Act and other country-specific laws.[3]

- Streamlining corporate tax codes (such as those in the USA) to facilitate capital upgrades to more energy-efficient equipment.[4]

---

1   Removing price subsidies in China, India, Indonesia, Iran, Russia, Kazakhstan, South Africa and Venezuela alone would reduce global energy usage by an estimated 3.5 per cent and reduce global CO_2 emissions by 4.6 per cent. International Energy Agency, *World Energy Outlook: Looking at Energy Subsidies*, Paris, 1999, pp. 9–10.

2   Peter Huber, 'The Four Hour Energy Crisis', *Forbes*, 17 September 2001, p. 88.

3   James Hansen has formally calculated that 'halting the growth of air pollution can make a significant contribution to slowing global warming'. Hansen, 'A Brighter Future', *Climate Change* 52, 2002, p. 435. Hansen, the father of the global warming alarm with his testimony on the subject to the US Senate in 1988, offered his analysis as an alternative to the 'doom and gloom scenario' (ibid., p. 435).

4   Government-mandated energy efficiency, on the other hand, is not a win-win proposition because the firm (or individual) is being forced to accept the believed-to-be value proposition. Energy service companies offering total outsourcing at guaranteed energy savings, the largest of which was Enron, were generally unprofitable, suggesting that *economic* energy savings were less than thought. Reasons why economic efficiency can diverge from engineering efficiency include transaction or 'hassle' costs of employing new technologies, hidden risks of using new technology, and the ingrained preferences of consumers. See IPCC, *Climate Change 2001: Mitigation*, op. cit., p. 507, and, generally, Frank Wirl, *The Economics of Conservation Programs*, Kluwer Academic Publishers, Boston, MA, 1997.

- Removing non-market barriers to increase the amount of electricity generated by nuclear power and hydropower, the two largest energy sources that do not emit carbon.
- Liberalising developing-country economies to reduce primitive biomass usage that produces soot aerosols, which are thought to be a global warming agent.[5]
- Ending debate on prospective cap-and-trade programmes (such as those in the USA) to remove the (mal)incentive for firms to postpone cost-effective GHG emissions reductions to achieve a higher baseline for future emissions.

Corporations may adopt policies to reduce GHG emissions as part of their own no-regrets climate policy. Such reductions, if they are truly voluntary, would not penalise consumers or shareholders; they would make financial sense by increasing efficiency (economic, not engineering), and/or complying with air pollution or toxic emission requirements. A broader part of a true no-regrets policy would include strictures against corporate 'rent-seeking' where firms seek mandatory GHG restraints for competitive advantage over their business rivals.[6]

A no-regrets approach should not be promoted as 'insurance' for a climate-change 'problem'. Not even the Kyoto Protocol reductions – which in the aggregate are beyond what the political system can deliver – can claim to be a climate insurance policy. The protocol is not a cure for man-made 'global warming' since the emissions reductions would result in a non-measurable impact

---

5   Sato et al., op. cit., p. 6,324.
6   For a case against corporate activism beyond 'no regrets', see Robert Bradley, 'Climate Alarmism and Corporate Responsibility', *Electricity Journal*, August/September 2000, pp. 65–71.

on global climate change for decades. Kyoto should be seen as an institution-building framework that would facilitate far greater restraints on self-interested market outcomes in the future than it does now. Yet the Kyoto agreement, if it is implemented and meets its targets, has costs that are far in excess of benefits according to macroeconomic modelling. In contrast to binding international agreements, the presidencies of George H. W. Bush and George W. Bush have tended towards a no-regrets policy for the US economy. The result has been energy growth and GHG emission increases of around 1.5 per cent per year.[7]

Beyond 'no regrets': a little something?

There is much interest in addressing such a large commons issue as anthropogenic climate change by 'doing something'. Often the middle ground is claimed by those who propose implementing a 'modest' carbon tax either directly, or indirectly through an air permit-trading scheme. Should public policy supplement 'no regrets' volunteerism with at least a modicum of activist climate policy in order to gain experience and set up the institutions in case additional measures are needed in the future?

---

7   President George H. W. Bush's intent to return US emissions to 1990 levels by 2000 was voluntary and subject to economic viability. At the end of 2000, emissions were 14 per cent above 1990 levels, an annual growth rate of 1.3 per cent (USA Energy Information Administration, *Emissions of Greenhouse Gases in the United States 2000*, DOE/EIA-0573, 9 November 2001). President George W. Bush has rejected the Kyoto Protocol's assignment for the USA to reduce GHG emissions 7 per cent below 1990 levels between 2008 and 2012 in the face of a Department of Energy estimate that US GHG emissions will be 36 per cent above 1990 levels by 2010 and 54 per cent higher by 2020, a 1.5 per cent annual increase (US Energy Information Administration, *International Energy Outlook 2002*, Government Printing Office, Washington, DC, 2002, p. 189).

The Nordhaus/Boyer proposal

Prominent economists William Nordhaus and Joseph Boyer have developed an integrated assessment model that leads them to reject the Kyoto Protocol and propose a modest unilateral tax in its place. A short-run tax of $5–10 per ton of carbon, which would have a total cost of $100 billion, is found to reduce emissions to create a net present value benefit of $300 billion (a 3:1 benefit/cost ratio). Assuming a year 2100 warming of 2.4°C, the temperature reduction would be 0.06°C (to 2.34°C), a 2.5 per cent decrease from business-as-usual.[8]

The above finding rests on an admittedly flawed assumption: that of perfect private-sector knowledge and perfect public-sector knowledge and policy implementation. The Nordhaus/Boyer optimal policy is assumed to follow a century-long 'where efficient, when efficient and why efficient' trajectory whereby authorities will make continual adjustments to ensure that the carbon tax is optimal at all times. Thus the world is one complete trading market. The carbon tax is set to a known environmental 'shadow price' to remove externalities. No political deviations occur.[9] Any frictions of transaction costs, tax and regulatory policy differentials, trade restrictions and obstacles to carbon trading credit from sinks are absent.[10]

This wholly unrealistic framework indicates that the 'market failure' at issue is so small that imperfect knowledge and government failure fritter away the aforementioned net benefit. As Nordhaus and Boyer clearly acknowledge, their finding of net benefits

---

8   Nordhaus and Boyer, *Warming the World*, op. cit., pp. 174–76.

9   Ibid., p. 123.

10   William Nordhaus, 'Global Warming Economics', *Science*, 9 November 2001, p. 1,283.

from a carbon tax is a theoretical construct only – a 'benchmark' with which to compare other (sub-optimal) policies. The authors do not mean for their 'optimal policy' to be a real-world policy directive as if 'an environmental pope will suddenly appear to provide infallible canons of policy that will be scrupulously followed by all'.[11] Yet the authors leave the obvious question unanswered: what would a realistic benefit/cost ratio be given an imperfect political system?

Cap-and-trade

A 'cap-and-trade' programme for CO_2 is moving towards implementation in the EU but facing stiff resistance in the USA. Yet US policy activists pragmatically favour this option over carbon taxes despite some important advantages of the latter, examined below.[12] Such a programme would allocate emission credits within a geographical area and let firms that are best able to reduce emissions trade with companies that need to emit more than their 'baseline' allocation. Voluntary programmes to establish early credit for future trading have been supported as a prelude to a mandatory one to encourage short-term action.[13]

A number of critical questions come to mind. What should the 'baseline' level of emissions be for different companies and

---

11 Nordhaus and Boyer, *Warming the World*, op. cit., p. 123.
12 Raymond Kopp et al., 'A Proposal for Credible Early Action in US Climate Policy', available at <www.weathervane.rff.org>.
13 See, generally, Robert Nordhaus et al., *Early Action & Global Climate Change: An Analysis of Early Action Crediting Proposal*, Pew Center on Global Climate Change, October 1998.

industries and for transportation versus stationary energy users to avoid economic and competitive distortions? In other words, how can the initial allocation of emission rights be 'efficient' and 'fair'? How can business-as-usual emission reductions (called 'anyway tons' by critics) be differentiated from 'real' incremental cuts? Will power generated from hydro and nuclear plants count in whole or part as credits? Specifically, how will hydro imports from Canada into the USA or nuclear imports from France into the UK be treated?

Once the initial allocation is made, can timely modifications – modifications that will necessarily impose capital gains and losses on participants – be made? What credit will be given for carbon sinks given the large uncertainty and slow evolution of knowledge regarding the carbon cycle? And finally, while trading programmes gain efficiencies over larger geographical regions, any new trading programme creates incentives for neighbouring regions not to participate to escape the artificially imposed costs.[14]

Is a cap-and-trade programme more efficient than a carbon tax programme given a mandate to reduce GHGs? A trading programme locks in large economic rents to producers of GHG credits, whereas a tax is more easily adjustable to new information – information that will surely change in an area as uncertain as

14 'Tradable permit regimes tend to resist policy changes of any sort, since changes impose capital gains and losses on those with long or short positions in permits. In addition, as many studies have shown, any geographically limited regime would induce investment in CO_2-intensive activities in non-participating nations, and the owners of those investments would be new opponents of their nations' participation.' Richard Schmalensee, 'Greenhouse Policy Architectures and Institutions', in William Nordhaus (ed.), *Economics and Policy Issues in Climate Change*, Resources for the Future, Washington, DC, 1998, pp. 147–48.

anthropogenic climate change. A tax is transparent for democratic decision-making whereas the consumer cost of trading values can only be approximated by specialists. A tax is also administratively simpler to implement and monitor whereas a trading programme will require a specialised bureaucracy. International cooperation may be easier with tax regimes than trading programmes as well.[15]

If these points have merit, political expediency in favour of cap-and-trade is another reason to avoid mandates entirely. The rent-seeking that causes many special interest groups to support cap-and-trade policies must be seen for what it is: a mechanism that amplifies the costs of such a policy, while doing nothing to produce real benefits.

Beyond 'no regrets': a lot of something?

Pursuant to the Kyoto Protocol and an alarmist interpretation of climate science, the EU is moving towards a carbon suppression policy despite two obstacles: 'end-user energy prices in the European Union are among the highest in the world, and it is widely regarded as politically perilous to raise taxes further'.[16] Motor fuel prices in Europe, led by the UK, for example, are several times higher than in the US, as seen in Figure 18.

The International Energy Agency (IEA) forecasts a 25 per cent increase in energy demand in OECD Europe by 2030 with carbon

---

15   On the advantages of a tax over cap-and-trade, see Bruce Stram, 'A Carbon Tax Strategy for Global Climate Change', in Henry Lee (ed.), *Shaping National Responses to Climate Change: A Post-Rio Guide*, Island Press, Washington, DC, 1995, pp. 219–35.

16   International Energy Agency, *World Energy Outlook 2002*, op. cit., p. 182.

Figure 18 **World petrol taxes**
1Q 2003, US$ per litre

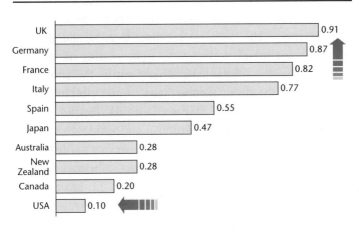

Note: US gallon = 3.8 litres
Source: International Energy Agency, *Energy Prices and Taxes, First Quarter 2003*, 2003.

emissions increasing by 23 per cent.[17] The congruency between energy usage and GHG emissions follows from the IEA's expectation that 'fossil fuels will continue to dominate the energy mix'.[18] The IEA's expectation in its prior (2000) report – 'continuing steady growth in world energy use and in related CO_2 emissions, despite the recent efforts by many OECD countries to mitigate unwanted climate change'[19] – continues to hold true.

Compared with the EU's commitment to reduce (and maintain) its greenhouse gas emissions to 8 per cent below 1990 levels in 2008–12, the IEA projects that emissions will be 10 per cent

17   Ibid., pp. 430, 433.

18   Ibid., p. 3.

19   Ibid.

above 1990 levels by 2030 and rising at an annual rate of 0.7 per cent – well above the 1971–2000 growth rate of 0.2 per cent per year.[20] Meanwhile, the European Environment Agency reports that aggregate GHG emissions increased in 2000 and again in 2001, 'moving the EU further away from meeting its commitment to achieve a substantial emissions cut by the 2008–2012 period'. Ten of the fifteen Member States are on a substantial non-compliance path – Austria, Belgium, Denmark, Finland, Greece, Ireland, Italy, the Netherlands, Portugal, and Spain.[21]

It is no secret that still-higher energy prices are needed to discourage consumption as a necessary but not sufficient condition for EU movement towards Kyoto compliance. EU Environment Commissioner Margot Wallström noted: 'Increasing energy prices is of course something that we should not leave to the oil producing countries. A well planned policy for energy taxation is the way forward.' Addressing the distortion that higher energy prices would cause in the EU relative to the rest of the world, she added: 'This is about international relations. This is about economy, about trying to create a level playing field for big businesses throughout the world. You have to understand what is at stake and that is why it is serious.'[22]

Her opinion was widely reported in the US press to indicate not only the anti-consumer nature of Kyoto but also to display the 'hurt one, hurt all' sentiment that lurked behind its advocacy.

Commissioner Wallström has disputed the benefits of lower

20 Ibid., pp. 192–93, 433.
21 European Environment Agency, 'EU Greenhouse Gas Emissions Rise for Second Straight Year', 6 May 2003, available at <http://org.eea.eu.int/documents/newsreleases/ghg-2003-en>.
22 Stephen Castle, 'EU Sends Strong Warning to Bush Over Greenhouse Gas Emissions', *Independent*, 19 March 2001, p. 14.

electricity prices stemming from the EU's power market deregulation policies: 'How can we expect electricity users to invest in more efficient machines, appliances or lighting systems when electricity is getting cheaper?' She warns, 'Those member states that currently resist higher energy taxes may soon come to understand that without them they will have difficulties to achieve their Kyoto targets.'[23] The EU all-pain-no-gain commitment to carbon suppression could not be clearer.

Also basing its premise on an alarmist interpretation of the science, the UK has embraced the EU goal of reducing GHG emissions by 60 per cent by 2050 from 1990 levels with a 12.5 per cent reduction by 2008–12 and a 20 per cent reduction by 2020. The policy implications of this include: a government-sponsored increase in the market share of renewables for power generation (from the present 3 per cent) to 10 per cent by 2010 and 20 per cent by 2020; carbon emission trading (as part of an EU plan); and the in-place Climate Change Levy.[24]

Major doubts have already been expressed about the GHG reduction targets and the ability of renewable energy, given the opposition to new nuclear facilities, to substitute for gas and coal in electricity generation. Ian Fells, writing for the Adam Smith Institute, calculated what such an effort would really mean:

> If all the wind farms currently operating in the world were to be put on the South Downs, assuming planning permission could be obtained, they would generate only *15 per cent of UK electricity*! To produce 20 per cent of UK electricity, largely

23 'Energy Taxes Must Rise to Save Climate – EU's Wallstrom', Reuters, 4 February 2001, reported at http://www.cei.org/gencon/014,02796.cfm.

24 Secretary of State for Trade and Industry, *Our Carbon Future – Creating a Low Carbon Economy*, Stationery Office, London, 2003, pp. 3, 8, 12, 25, 29, 46.

from wind, would require twenty 2MW machines to be installed every week between now and 2020, most of them offshore.[25]

Looking then to biomass, given a paucity of untapped hydro sites in the UK, Fells found that 'a little arithmetic shows that the whole of Kent would have to be turned over to coppiced willow to replace half the output of Dungeness B nuclear power station on the Kent coast'. His conclusion: the 20 per cent target is 'high risk' and 'irresponsible'.[26]

Perception over reality has become a staple of the energy sustainability debate. During the Clinton era, US Department of Energy (DOE) Secretary Bill Richardson predicted that wind could supply 5 per cent of US electricity by 2020 – a 125-fold increase. Yet at the same time the independent forecasting arm of DOE, the Energy Information Administration, put the estimate at 0.08 per cent for 2020, still a doubling from 2000 levels.[27] Royal Dutch Shell generated favourable publicity by predicting that renewable energy could satisfy 50 per cent of worldwide energy demand by mid-century.[28] These quixotic forecasts will probably be long forgotten as their due dates near.

25 Ian Fells, 'A Cloudy Energy Future', Adam Smith Institute, 24 February 2002, p. 3. Available at http://www.adamsmith.org/policy/publications/pdf-files/fells-energy.pdf.

26 Ibid., p. 3.

27 US Department of Energy, 'Richardson Unveils National Wind Energy Initiative', *DOE News*, 21 June 1999; US Energy Information Administration, *Annual Energy Outlook 2001*, Department of Energy, Washington, DC, 2000, pp. 129, 150. The report added (p. 79): 'High capital costs, lower output per kilowatt, and intermittent availability are expected to continue to disadvantage wind power relative to conventional generating technologies.'

28 Organisation for Economic Cooperation and Development, *Sustainable Development: Critical Issues*, Paris, 2001, p. 342.

What really would happen if the EU reduced GHG emissions by 60 per cent by 2050? Onshore nuclear plants and offshore wind turbines would be commonplace. High levels of intermittent generation might cause lights to flicker – and much worse. Energy usage pared by high prices would leave manufacturing non-competitive and living standards lower. All this would contradict the promises in the February 2003 UK Energy White Paper that a 'move to a new, low carbon economy' would not compromise liberalisation, competitiveness, innovation, reliability, and a 'clear and stable policy framework'.[29]

Could William Stanley Jevons's alarmism towards coal depletion in 1865 apply to energy in general in the EU in 2050? 'The exhaustion of our mines will be marked *pari passu* by a rising cost or value of coal,' he warned, 'and when the price has risen to a certain amount comparatively to the price in other countries, our main branches of trade will be doomed.'[30] The winners in the 21st century would be the USA and many developing nations welcoming the benefits of carbon-based energies.

Environmentalist/environmental regret

The human influence on climate has become the main issue of the modern environmental movement. The question of whether or not policy reform can have a demonstrable effect on future climate is lost amid the zeal to constrain economic expansion and foster green sinks where carbon is sequestered from the atmosphere by biomass uptake in the short run. Source-and-sink (emission and

---

29   Secretary of State for Trade and Industry, op. cit., pp. 3, 28, 95.

30   Jevons, op. cit., p. 57.

uptake) planning to 'stabilise climate' has replaced central macro-economic planning as the 'commanding heights' of the economy for a new intellectual elite – and, to use F. A. Hayek's phrase, a potential 'road to serfdom'.

Not surprisingly, this very complicated issue has introduced a set of trade-offs and unintended consequences for traditional environmentalists – and also for the environment itself.

Hydro and nuclear power

The most immediate problem of the Kyoto carbon suppression crusade for many environmentalists is the revitalised rationale for nuclear power and hydropower as continuing primary energy sources. Both are currently the only large-scale energy alternatives to electricity generated by oil, natural gas and coal. Yet most environmentalists somewhat arbitrarily and hypocritically have judged the negative characteristics of nuclear and hydropower to outweigh their emission-free advantages.

In 2001, 155 times more grid electricity was produced in the USA from nuclear and hydro sources than from solar and wind facilities combined.[31] For OECD Europe, nearly 70 times more power was generated from nuclear and hydro sources than from all solar and wind facilities combined.[32] Consequently, environmentalist attempts to retire existing hydro and nuclear capacity and block new projects raise the question of trade-offs with air emissions policy. Success at blocking power production from

---

31 US Energy Information Administration, *Annual Energy Review 2001*, op. cit., p. 225.

32 International Energy Agency, *World Energy Outlook 2002*, op. cit., pp. 431–32.

these sizeable sources may more than offset the GHG (and air pollution) savings from their preferred energy sources, leaving the Kyoto reduction targets even less practical than before for the protocol's proponents.

Kyoto compromises

The Kyoto Protocol has been so compromised that some environmentalists have asked whether circumvention and opportunism could ruin the whole effort. Christopher Flavin of the Worldwatch Institute complained in a 'candid assessment' in 1998, 'The challenge now is to renovate the baroque structure that the Kyoto Protocol has become – or else scrap it and get ready to start over.'[33] Yet two years later, after the Kyoto Protocol was weakened again to attract more international support (Kyoto-Bonn Accord), Flavin and others rallied around the protocol as the only game in town.[34] Today's pragmatism could, however, diminish if the regulatory/ political effort is perceived as promoting corporate welfare within a business-as-usual framework rather than resulting in real incremental GHG emission cutbacks. Environmentalists may conclude, as Björn Lomborg did,[35] that wholly new priorities are needed to redirect resources to higher-value issues, environmental and non-environmental.

33 Christopher Flavin, 'Last Tango in Buenos Aires', *Worldwatch*, November/ December 1998, pp. 11, 18.
34 Worldwatch Institute News Release, 'The World Cannot Wait for Another Treaty', 28 March 2001.
35 'Prioritization is absolutely essential if we are to achieve the best possible distribution of resources in society. The environment must participate in this social prioritization on equal terms with all other areas.' Lomborg, op. cit., p. 348.

Emission trade-offs

Emission trade-offs exist between CO_2 and some pollutants. Diesel fuel emits more air pollutants but less carbon dioxide emissions than reformulated gasoline on a per-kilometre basis. Yet unlike their European counterparts, US environmentalists have railed against the very concept of 'green diesel' in favour of gasoline – and have thus acquiesced to the higher CO_2 emissions from such a policy.[36] On the other hand, if diesel black carbon is a global warming agent, the trade-off may be less pronounced.

On the power generation side, increasing environmentalist opposition to natural gas drilling in 'sensitive' areas is likely to have unintended air emission consequences.[37] The USA has far greater indigenous coal than natural gas resources in absolute terms and relative to consumption. It exports about 4 per cent of its annual coal production and imports around 16 per cent of its gas usage on a net basis.[38] Gas imports are typically capacity constrained, leaving domestic storage as the main mechanism of ensuring that supply can respond to short-term changes in demand. Thus access restrictions to prime drilling areas affect the supply and price of

---

36 Marla Cone, 'Dirty Exhaust: America's Unhealthy Reliance on Diesel', *Los Angeles Times*, 30 May 1999, p. A1; Thomas J. Lueck, 'Environmentalists Assail Plan to Add Diesel Buses', *New York Times*, 2 January 2000, p. 25.

37 'We see two levels of opposition [to natural gas drilling] in [Colorado]. One comes from vocal, organized, anti-development environmental groups whose mission in life is to stop gas drilling. Five years ago, their mission was to stop coal-fired generation and replace it with gas-fired power. Today that has gone out the door, and now they are opposing gas drilling.' Greg Schnacke, executive vice-president, Colorado Oil & Gas Association, quoted in Dan Holder, 'Rockies Working to Develop Natural Gas Resources', *Oil & Gas Reporter*, July 2002, p. 163.

38 US Energy Information Administration, *Annual Energy Review 2001*, op. cit., pp. 181, 201.

natural gas more than coal for power generation in the USA.

While the major public policy issue for the coal industry is climate change alarmism, the major issue for natural gas is access to new reserves. The National Petroleum Council estimated in a 1999 study that 15 per cent of the estimated domestic US gas resource base is subject to outright or partial access constraints.[39] This means that future gas production can be more easily blocked, which is likely to increase coal burning and the emissions therefrom – at least until a global LNG (liquefied natural gas) market with greater takeaway capacity on the US side develops.

Another practical problem for many environmentalists is the failure to consider the 'opportunity cost' of money spent on improving the environment. The current focus of energy reformers is to maximise subsidies and mandates for 'emission-free' electricity generation capacity from wind and solar. Yet if the resources to be spent on environmental improvements are scarce, the same resources could go to emission reductions at the dirtiest carbon-energy-fired plants. Seen in this way, a new solar or wind farm has an environmental opportunity cost and may even be a net polluter.

Renewable trade-offs

Land-intensive non-hydro renewable capacity creates, to adapt a phrase used in other areas of the environmental debate, *energy urban sprawl*, whereby pristine areas, in addition to the renewable energy structures themselves, are 'industrialised' with roads and transmission lines to demand centres that are often far away. This

---

39 National Petroleum Council, *Natural Gas: Meeting the Challenges of the Nation's Growing Natural Gas Demand*, 3 vols, Washington, DC, December 1999, vol. 1, pp. 12–13.

has been an environmental issue for years and is growing. A US study in 1999 concluded:

> Environmental organizations generally support the development of 'renewable' energy resources ... but reserve judgment on specific projects until site-specific impacts are known. Depending on local conditions, environmental criticism of renewable plants can be every bit as scathing as for fossil plants, much to the dismay of policy advocates.[40]

A *New York Times* article in mid-2003 reported that proposed US wind farm projects, inland and offshore, have created 'huge turbulence with the environmental movement'. The article continued, 'The growing [wind] industry has caused a kind of identity crisis among people who think of themselves as pro-environment, forcing them to choose between the promise of clean, endlessly renewable energy and the perils of imposing giant man-made structures on nature.'[41] A highly publicised debate over a proposed 420-megawatt project off the coast of southern New England (powered by GE turbines that stand 100 metres tall on land and 72–75 metres offshore) has pitted local against national environmentalists. Asks one writer: 'Will the real environmentalist please stand up?'[42]

It remains to be seen how many offshore wind farms, in particular, will be built in developed countries before a critical mass

40 Rich Ferguson, 'Electric Industry Restructuring and Environmental Stewardship', *Electricity Journal*, July 1999, pp. 27–28.
41 Katherine Seelye, 'Windmill Farms Sow Environmentalists' Identity Crisis', *New York Times*, 5 June 2003, p. A22.
42 Elisa Wood, 'The US Offshore Wind Market', *Renewable Energy World*, May/June 2003, p. 54.

of (environmental) opposition coalesces. If more and more economically workable areas for renewable projects are deemed too 'sensitive', will major renewable farms or sites effectively turn into 'depletable' resources? Hydroelectricity has already reached that point in some developed countries such as the USA and the UK.

Solar applications have a market niche in small remote areas that are far from the power grid. Little carbon energy is displaced, and, in fact, solar would serve as a *bridge energy* to carbon fuels once the remote area is developed.

Within areas served by a power grid, at least in the USA, solar energy is popular for hot tubs and swimming pools, which has raised environmental angst.[43] Offshore oil platforms use solar panels. One of the largest solar facilities in the USA powers the recovery of heavy crude oil.[44] Solar, in its present use, is as much a *complement* as a substitute for the carbon energy.

Geothermal sites, where usable energy can be derived from heat generated within the earth itself, are concentrated in the western USA and are restricted to a limited range of countries. Many untapped sites are considered to be in 'sensitive' areas. Turning to the two largest renewables, hydropower and primitive biomass, a sustainability issue has been raised by the IPCC:

43 'I bring the [solar] industry from all over the country to meet with [US Environmental Protection Agency Administrator] Carol [Browner] [including] … the biggest solar pool heating company. They go around talking about what they do. And [Browner] is stonefaced. … And she goes "I hate swimming pools." And he goes, "Why?" And she goes, "Well, they're just vats of chemicals."' Scott Sklar, Solar Energy Industry Association, quoted in Joseph Schuler Jr, 'Let's Schmooze', *Public Utilities Fortnightly*, 15 April 1998, p. 37.

44 ChevronTexaco, *Up to the Challenge: 2002 Annual Report*, p. 23. This is not the first time renewables have aided the hydrocarbon age. William Stanley Jevons reported in 1865 that 'in 1708 windmills were wanted to try and drain certain Scotch coal-mines'. Jevons, op. cit., p. 75.

> Renewable technologies are not always sustainable in
> the sense of being socially and environmentally benign.
> Particularly in the case of large-scale applications in
> developing countries, notably of hydropower and biomass,
> adverse effects may arise for the local population. Moreover,
> adverse environmental side effects may occur, such as smog
> from the use of traditional biomass fuels … or changes in
> biological habitats and local climate.[45]

Will 'pro'-renewables policies such as mandates increasingly collide with other environmental values in the future? Major governmental energy forecasts, as mentioned above, identify environmental constraints with renewables as a factor contributing to an increased market share for carbon energies in the next twenty to thirty years.[46] Some voices in the mainstream environmental community are also – slowly but surely – reconsidering the practicality, efficacy and fairness of an anti-petroleum energy policy for the developing world.[47]

The environmentalists' tie to non-hydro renewables has extended to the transportation side. Ethanol (ethyl alcohol), produced from grain (mainly corn) and some waste products, produces a high-octane motor fuel when blended with 15 per cent

---

45 IPCC, *Climate Change 1995: Economic and Social Dimensions*, p. 241.

46 See pp. 33–4.

47 'Does it make sense to ask the poor to take on novel devices and fuels that have never been tried elsewhere? … Rather than excluding petroleum some of this one-time gift from nature ought actually to be reserved to help fulfill our obligation to bring the health and welfare of all people to a reasonable level: an essential goal of sustainable development, no matter how defined.' Kirk Smith, 'In Praise of Petroleum?', *Science*, 6 December 2002, p. 184. Also see, generally, Jack Hollander, *The Real Environmental Crisis: Why Poverty, Not Affluence, Is the Environment's Number One Enemy*, University of California Press, Los Angeles, CA, 2003.

gasoline (E85). Yet this renewable may be less environmentally friendly than petrol. Ethanol displaces petrol at the pump but consumes a good deal of energy (primarily diesel for cultivating farmland and processing grain) to produce a low net energy gain. Ethanol also emits much of the same ozone-forming emissions and CO_2 as pure gasoline.[48] Some environmentalists have opposed ethanol for these reasons. Others have supported ethanol to preserve the political unity of renewables and as an oxygenate with lower benzene, toluene and xylene emissions.

A technological fix?

Environmentalists have not only put nuclear and hydropower back into play; they have inspired great interest in addressing the carbon cycle through absorption to allow business-as-usual emission paths for carbon energies. Carbon energy critic John Holden, a technological optimist for a low-carbon-energy economy, turns pessimistic when mitigation is offered as an alternative to prevention:

'Geotechnical engineering' … suffer[s] too much from insufficient understanding of the intricacies of the planet's climatic machinery for us to be confident of achieving the desired effects (or, to be more confident of doing more good than harm). Humans are powerful enough to disrupt the climate and smart enough to notice we are doing it, but

---

48 Hosein Shapouri et al. ('The Energy Balance of Corn Ethanol: An Update', US Department of Agriculture, July 2002, p. iii) calculated a 34 per cent net energy gain, but David Pimentel ('Limits of Biomass Utilization', *Encyclopedia of Physical Science and Technology*, September 2001, pp. 159–71), using greatly different assumptions, gave ethanol a negative energy value.

we are not yet competent enough to fine-tune the complex
machinery of climate to our tastes. The possibilities – and
the climate system itself – need much more study.[49]

Yet serious efforts to equilibrate the carbon cycle will have to employ novel sequestration strategies given increasing energy usage,
supply constraints with renewable energies and political and economic limitations with nuclear power.

Holdren cannot have it both ways. If he sounds the climate
alarm, he should welcome open-ended research programmes to
uncover ways to balance the carbon cycle at a cost that is competitive with the limited option of carbon suppression. If he wants to
plead ignorance about the 'intricacies' of climate to forestall high-
technology solutions, he should also acknowledge the limits to
understanding the intricacies of the anthropogenic influence on
climate – *and* the economic and social effects of moving away
from carbon energies. The science of climate change, not only
geo-engineering, requires further study. Modelling studies have
found that delaying policy activism by a decade or more has a surprisingly low cost – and a much lower cost than implementing an
inefficient policy programme.[50]

High-technology carbon energies – clean diesel, clean coal and
low-emission gasoline – improve the environment and extend the
carbon energy age. 'Green' energy companies such as bp and Royal
Dutch Shell are increasing the sustainability of carbon energies by

49 Holdren, 'Memorandum to the President: The Energy-Climate Challenge', op.
    cit., p. 33. Geo-engineering ranges from capturing carbon upon combustion to
    creating artificial sinks to retire carbon emissions.

50 Nordhaus and Boyer, *Warming the World*, op. cit., p. 174.

their actions even as they publicly speak of a post-carbon-energy age. Reality is working on many fronts and in subtle ways in favour of conventional energies.

Corporatism (corporate welfare)

The left has traditionally been a watchdog over government/ business relations and wary of corporate welfare. While a decade or more ago most leading wind and solar companies were small outfits full of youthful idealism, today's leaders, such as bp (solar) and GE (wind), are among the largest companies in the world. Shell has also carried the renewable energy banner in recent years. Critics such as Greenpeace have raised the hue of 'greenwashing' since bp and Shell are overwhelmingly conventional energy companies whose global hunt for oil and gas reserves and downstream investments are extending the carbon energy age.[51] *The Economist* is not being fooled either when it entitles an article dissecting bp's positioning in Russia's huge oil and gas industry as 'Not Beyond Petroleum'.[52]

bp, Shell and GE will continue to exploit renewable markets for public relations purposes as long as some combination of taxpayer and ratepayer subsidies permits them to tolerate losses or endure low returns, which are endemic to the wind and solar market.

Will environmentalists continue to sanctify government mandates and tax subsidies to oil majors and mega-conglomerates for their tepid investments in politically favoured energy projects?

51   Sharon Beder, *Global Spin: The Corporate Assault on the Environment*, Chelsea Green, White River Junction, VT, 2002, p. 265.

52   Staff article, 'Not Beyond Petroleum', *Economist*, 15 February 2003, p. 58.

Some on the left believe that corporations are getting the best of environmentalists in the partnership and want to start again. Sharon Beder states:

> In the end, despite bp's rhetoric about social responsibility, triple bottom lines and enlightened self interest, profits seem to count most. An oil company might invest in solar energy and admit that global warming should be prevented, but it will do all it can to ensure it can go on drilling for fossil fuels and expanding its markets for them.[53]

She concludes:

> A new wave of environmentalism is called for: one that will engage in the task of exposing corporate myths and methods of manipulation. One that opens up new areas and ideas to public debate rather than following an old agenda set by corporations.[54]

Conclusion

Public policy is not often seen in terms of black and white, but the climate issue might be an exception. 'Doing a little something' and 'getting started' with such things as a CO_2 cap-and-trade programme are not cost-effective and cannot appreciably address, even in subsequent iterations, the problems they are intended to solve. The small beginnings, however, create the institutional structure that will lead to environmental activism not justified by

---

53 Sharon Beder, 'bp: Beyond Petroleum?', in Eveline Lubbers (ed.), *Battling Big Business*, Common Courage Press, Monroe, ME, 2002, p. 32.

54 Beder, *Global Spin*, op. cit., p. 285.

either economics or environmentalism. Small steps, like potentially larger ones, will impact most heavily on the poorest nations and the poorest citizens of the wealthiest countries. Attention is diverted from the real root of energy and economic sustainability problems – *statism*. The over-arching goal of mandatory carbon constraint also siphons resources from dealing with current environmental problems and creates 'collateral damage' for other environmental ends. It remains to be seen whether or not these issues lead to a reconsideration of priorities.

7 CONCLUSIONS

Today's carbon-based energy economy is rapidly evolving for the better. The global resource base and substitutability are expanding. New avenues for consumption are multiplying. Reliability is improving. Energy intensity is dropping. Air and water pollution are declining. Wastage is falling. And where markets have been allowed to operate, energy has become more affordable over time.

The increasing anthropogenic influence on global climate does not negate the above positive developments. Climate optimists-qua-realists welcome carbon energies not only for their intended consequences but also for some of their unintended consequences – carbon fertilisation, proportionately higher minimum temperatures, longer growing seasons and a more active hydrologic cycle. A moderately warmer, wetter world – whether its causes are natural and/or anthropogenic – is likely to be a better world.

Time will enable energy-rich societies and new technologies to address carbon cycle imbalances if it ever becomes necessary. With or without a future 'carbon problem', technology will work to directly mitigate weather extremes and help individuals adapt to the perennial challenge of inclement weather and shifting climate patterns.

The challenge of energy sustainability is *political*, not economic or environmental. Government intervention makes energy artificially scarce and expensive and disrupts the natural improvement process. Seen in this light, the major challenge to energy sustainability is the international political movement to cap carbon emissions in the quixotic quest to 'stabilise' the climate.

Six complementary realities will continue or increase the predicament of anti-carbon environmentalism over time.

- Carbon energies will continue to improve relative to politically favoured substitutes that have greater shortcomings.
- Rising consumer expectations in democratic settings will limit the political ability to reduce GHG emissions via higher prices and inconvenience.
- The moral and economic imperative for the developing countries to industrialise will accelerate carbon energy usage (as predicted by the US Department of Energy and the OECD's International Energy Agency).
- Global competition and industrialisation will reward those jurisdictions that implement policies that foster energy abundance relative to those that do not.
- Greenhouse gas emissions will continue to increase, but the dire problems predicted by climate alarmists will be difficult to isolate and attribute (much like today).
- Forced reductions of greenhouse gas emissions beyond 'no regrets' will be controversial, incremental and ultimately ineffectual. These problems on the surface may be political, but at root they are intellectual and practical.

Environmentalists should reconsider the public policies suggested by acceptance of the climate alarmism position. Energy poverty caused by artificial energy scarcity can only translate into economic and environmental poverty. Rich societies benefiting from market economies have the means to anticipate and ameliorate unfavourable weather events and fully capitalise on improving climatic conditions from the anthropogenic influence. One main conclusion emerges. The best environmental policy is the best energy and economic policy, which means a continuing primary role for carbon energies the world over in accordance with private property, voluntary exchange and consumer sovereignty.

APPENDIX A **FALSIFIED CARBON ENERGY ALARMISM**

A review of the track record of some of today's leading climate alarmists is illustrative for policy-makers and others in the climate change debate. Such a retrospective is also fair warning to all participants in the energy and energy-environmental debate to revisit their pessimism to ensure that problems are well matched with fiscal priorities (the central message of Björn Lomborg's book, *The Skeptical Environmentalist*).

The following quotations are taken from the writings of two leading American energy alarmists, Paul Ehrlich and John Holdren, and classified under different headings.

Depletion

A genuine world shortage of pumpable petroleum appears certain by the turn of the century *if* demand continues to grow as it did in the 1960s.

> Paul and Anne Ehrlich, *The End of Affluence*, Rivercity Press, Riverside, MA, 1974, 1975, p. 44

Most of the easily accessible sources of fossil fuels and mineral resources are long gone, and the rising prices reflect the necessity to dig deeper, travel farther, and refine lower-grade ore in order to obtain them.

> Ibid., p. 100

Today the frontiers are gone, and the evidence is mounting
that technology cannot hold the law of diminishing returns
at bay much longer. Resources being stressed today are
often being stressed globally; they will not be replenished
from outside the 'system'.

> John Holdren and Paul Ehrlich, 'Resource Realities', in Holdren and
> Ehrlich (eds), *Global Ecology*, Harcourt Brace Jovanovich,
> New York, 1971, p. 8

The rapacious depletion of our fossil fuels is already forcing
us to consider more expensive mining techniques to gain
access to lower-grade deposits, such as the oil shales, and
even the status of our high-grade uranium ore reserves is not
clear-cut.

> John Holdren and Paul Ehrlich, 'Population and Panaceas: A
> Technological Perspective', in Holdren and Ehrlich, op. cit., p. 18

Compared to what will occur if we do not start seriously
conserving energy – and compared to the food,
environmental, and economic crises soon to come – the
1973–74 energy shortage was truly only a mini-crisis.

> Paul and Anne Ehrlich, op. cit., pp. 48–49

We can be reasonably sure … that within the next quarter
of a century mankind will be looking elsewhere than in
oil wells for its main source of energy. … We can also be
reasonably sure that the search for alternatives will be a
frantic one.

> Ibid., p. 49

High-grade iron, copper, and other ores are no longer
easily accessible; nor does oil bubble to the surface. ... The
world is running short of vital resources, and the American
economic system must adjust to this reality.

> Paul Ehrlich, *The Population Bomb*, Buccaneer Books, Cutchogue,
> New York, 1968, 1971, pp. 48, 162

That we are presently living beyond our means is
obvious from the simple fact that we are madly depleting
nonreplenishable resources.

> Ibid., p. 145

Economists as a group have been guiltier than most in
perpetuating the most dangerous myths of this troubled
age ... Mineral economists rely on the cornucopian dream,
in which advancing technology conjures up ever cheaper
minerals while consuming ever increasing amounts of
energy and the earth's crust to do it.

> John Holdren and Paul Ehrlich, 'Prospects for a Sane Economics',
> in Holdren and Ehrlich, op. cit., p. 177

There is little reason to believe that energy will get cheaper.

> Paul Ehrlich, Anne Ehrlich and John Holdren, *Ecoscience: Population,
> Resources, and Environment*, W. H. Freeman, San Francisco,
> CA, 1977, p. 954

With respect to economic costs ... it is questionable
whether potential resources can be converted into available
supplies at economic costs society can pay.

> John Holdren, 'Energy Costs as Potential Limits to Growth', in
> Dennis Pirages (ed.), *The Sustainable Society: Implications for Limited
> Growth*, Praeger, New York, 1977, p. 53

As the geophysicist M. King Hubbert had argued already
in the 1950s, the rate of consumption will peak and begin
to decline when cumulative consumption reaches about
half the initial endowment – an event that can be expected
between 2010 and 2020.

> John Holdren, 'Population and the Energy Problem', *Population and
> Environment: A Journal of Interdisciplinary Studies*,
> spring 1991, pp. 244, 246

Both for the United States and for the world, any significant
increase in consumption of oil and gas will lead to the
substantial depletion of the recoverable resources of those
materials by early in the next century.

> Ehrlich, Ehrlich and Holdren, *Ecoscience*, op. cit., p. 403

The complexity, the expense, and the environmental impact
of exploratory drilling increase greatly as depletion of the
most accessible deposits pushes the search for oil and gas
into more remote and more hostile environments.

> Ibid., p. 413.

A major reason for the particularly rapid growth of energy
use per capita in the past two decades was that energy
was cheaper than what it replaced – human labor and
time, for example ... The cost of depleting the richest,
most accessible fossil fuels must now be paid in the form
of rapidly rising expenses for locating, extracting, and
processing the leaner and more remote deposits that
remain, and for developing and deploying sophisticated
technologies to harness less limited substitutes.

> Ibid., p. 484

By the 1980s, the depletion of accessible reserves of many
nonrenewable resources – notably, but not exclusively,

petroleum – was becoming more and more evident.

> Paul and Anne Ehrlich, *The Population Explosion*, Simon & Schuster,
> New York, 1990, p. 57

The problem is not that we are running out of energy. It's that we have nearly run out of the low-cost energy that has fueled the industrial development of today's rich countries and has shaped the expectations of the poor ones.

> Holdren, 'Population and the Energy Problem', op. cit., p. 232

Except for the huge pool of oil underlying the Middle East, the cheapest oil and gas are already gone. The trends that had kept costs down until the beginning of the 1970s in spite of cumulative depletion – new discoveries and economies of scale in processing and transport – have played themselves out.

> John Holdren, 'The Transition to Costlier Energy', in Lee Schipper,
> Stephen Meyers et al., *Energy Efficiency and Human Activity: Past, Trends,*
> *Future Prospects*, Cambridge University Press, Cambridge, 1992, pp. 9–10

Pollution

Los Angeles smog laws have just barely been able to keep pace with their increasing population of automobiles (the main source of LA smog). It seems unlikely that much improvement can be expected in this aspect of air pollution until a major shift in our economy takes place. As long as we have an automobile industry centered on the internal combustion engine and a social system which values large, overpowered cars as status symbols, we are likely to be in trouble.

> Ehrlich, *The Population Bomb*, op. cit., p. 103

Virtually every major metropolis in the world has an air pollution problem, and the rate of expansion of urban complexes everywhere is rapidly making the brown pall and smarting eyes ubiquitous symbols of 'progress'.

John Holdren and Paul Ehrlich, 'Environmental Roulette, Overpopulation and Potential for Ecocide', in Holdren and Ehrlich, *Global Ecology*, op. cit., p. 66

Our limited knowledge of the details of air pollution permits little hope for early relief.

Holdren and Ehrlich, 'Environmental Roulette', op. cit., p. 66

Climate change

We are not, of course, optimistic about our chances of success. Some form of ecocatastrophe, if not thermonuclear war, seems almost certain to overtake us before the end of the century. (The inability to forecast exactly which one – whether plague, famine, the poisoning of the oceans, drastic climatic change, or some disaster entirely unforeseen – is hardly grounds for complacency.)

John Holdren and Paul Ehrlich, 'What We Must Do, and the Cost of Failure', in Holdren and Ehrlich, *Global Ecology*, op. cit., p. 279

As University of California physicist John Holdren has said, it is possible that carbon-dioxide climate-induced famines could kill as many as a billion people before the year 2020.

Paul Ehrlich, *The Machinery of Nature*, Simon & Schuster, New York, 1986, p. 274

Long continuation of present trends has the potential for making us uncomfortably warm (if one degree does not trigger disaster, wait for a few more doubling times!).

John Holdren, 'Global Thermal Pollution', in Holdren and Ehrlich,
Global Ecology, op. cit., p. 88

Too much fossil fuel means flirtation with a CO_2-induced climate change potentially catastrophic for world food production.

John Holdren, 'Renewables in the US Energy Future: How Much,
How Fast?', *Energy* 6(9), 1981, p. 913

In the long run CO_2-induced warming would melt the polar ice caps, thus flooding many areas, putting New York City, Washington, DC, and Sacramento, California, under water. Much of eastern England and the low countries would be inundated, and millions of people would be forced by rising waters out of the Tokyo-Yokohama area of Japan. Bangladesh would become submerged, and Rangoon, Calcutta, and Buenos Aires would be gone. Florida would largely disappear, and much of the lower Mississippi River Valley would become an inland sea.

Robert Ornstein and Paul Ehrlich, *New World New Mind: Moving
Toward Conscious Evolution*, Doubleday, New York, 1989, pp. 77–78

Whether a global compact to reduce CO_2 emissions can be drafted in the near future may depend largely on the severity, over the next year or two, of weather anomalies plausibly attributable to global climate change.

John Holdren, 'The Transition to Costlier Energy', in Schipper,
Meyers et al., *Energy Efficiency*, op. cit., p. 42

I believe that most people – by which I mean not only most members of the public, most journalists, and most policy-makers, but also a great many natural scientists, social scientists, and technologists – continue to underestimate the problem of human-induced disruption of global climate.

John Holdren, 'Six Reasons to Take Action', *Foreign Service Journal*, March 1999, p. 21

Many observers have speculated that the [global] cooling could be the beginning of a long and persistent trend in that direction – that is, an inevitable departure from an abnormally warm period in climatic history.

Ehrlich, Ehrlich and Holdren, *Ecoscience*, op. cit., p. 686

There can be scant consolation in the idea that a man-made warming trend might cancel out a natural cooling trend. Since the different factors producing the two trends do so by influencing different parts of Earth's complicated climatic machinery, it is most unlikely that the associated effects on circulation patterns would cancel each other.

Ibid., p. 687

Conservation

Only one rational path is open to us – simultaneous de-development of the [overdeveloped countries] and semi-development of the [underdeveloped countries], in order to approach a decent and ecologically sustainable standard of living for all in between. By de-development we mean lower per-capita energy consumption, fewer gadgets, and the abolition of planned obsolescence.

John Holdren and Paul Ehrlich, 'Introduction', in Holdren and Ehrlich, *Global Ecology*, op. cit., p. 3

A massive campaign must be launched to restore a high-quality environment in North America and to de-develop the United States … Resources and energy must be diverted from frivolous and wasteful uses in overdeveloped countries to filling the genuine needs of underdeveloped countries. This effort must be largely political.

> John Holdren, Anne Ehrlich and Paul Ehrlich, *Human Ecology: Problems and Solutions*, W. H. Freeman, San Francisco, CA, 1973, p. 279

The United States could halve its energy consumption per person and enjoy a quality of life even higher than today's.

> Paul and Anne Ehrlich, *Extinction: The Causes and Consequences of the Disappearance of Species*, Random House, New York, 1981, p. 247

It is quite plausible that, using known technologies that would be effective at today's energy prices, the current US standard of living could be provided with about half the current US energy use per capita.

> Holdren, 'Population and the Energy Problem', op. cit., p. 237

Power plant impact

The American power industry wants to *increase* our per capita consumption at a rate that will double our national use of power every decade. At this rate, every square inch of the United States would be covered with conventional power plants in two hundred years or so.

> Paul Ehrlich and Richard Harriman, *How to Be a Survivor*, Rivercity Press, Rivercity, MA, 1971, 1975, p. 71

Except in special circumstances, all construction of power generating facilities should cease immediately, and power companies should be forbidden to encourage people to use more power. *Power is much too cheap.* It should certainly be made more expensive and perhaps rationed, in order to reduce its frivolous use.

Ibid., p. 72

By far the worst prospects, however, are those for the world's river systems. It is estimated that by 1985 fully one quarter of the total annual runoff by the United States will be for cooling tower plants.

John Holdren and Paul Ehrlich, 'Environmental Roulette, Overpopulation and Potential for Ecocide', in Holdren and Ehrlich, *Global Ecology*, op. cit., p. 69

Loss of freedom/central planning

It seems clear that the first major penalty man will have to pay for his rapid consumption of the earth's nonrenewable resources will be that of having to live in a world where his thoughts and actions are ever more strongly limited, where social organization has become all pervasive, complex, and inflexible, and where the state completely dominates the actions of the individual.

Harrison Brown (1954), quoted in Ehrlich, Ehrlich and Holdren, *Ecoscience*, op. cit., p. 388

[The] cost of energy supply [includes] ... undesirable social or political change (for example, loss of civil liberties as a part of government's response to technology-induced vulnerability).

Holdren, 'Energy Costs as Potential Limits to Growth', op. cit., p. 59

Policy

Many of the conservation measures temporarily undertaken when the mini-crisis was in its acute stage – lowered speed limits, car-pools, reset thermostats, etc. – should be instituted on a permanent basis … In the long run, energy should be made *expensive*, especially for large users, as an incentive to conservation.

Ehrlich and Ehrlich, *The End of Affluence*, op. cit., p. 48

Laws may well be passed strictly limiting the number of appliances a single family may possess.

Ehrlich and Harriman, *How to Be a Survivor*, op. cit., p. 69

Unnecessary lighting in offices and factories should … be banned.

Ehrlich and Ehrlich, *The End of Affluence*, op. cit., p. 226

It should immediately be made illegal to construct a building with windows which cannot be opened.

Ehrlich and Harriman, *How to Be a Survivor*, op. cit., pp. 73–74

Completely frivolous uses of power, such as gas yard lamps that are permanently lit, should be outlawed altogether.

Ehrlich and Ehrlich, *The End of Affluence*, op. cit., p. 227

APPENDIX B   IPCC SUPPORT FOR CLIMATE OPTIMISM

The latest scientific report from the Intergovernmental Panel on Climate Change (IPCC), a scientific committee organised by the United Nations to present the latest information to the public policy community and others, published in 2001, generally supports the high-sensitivity estimates of future warming from climate modelling as the basis for climate economics and public policy. Despite this bias, many findings of the report contradict an alarmist interpretation of the present and future anthropogenic influence on climate. The conclusions presented below should carry great weight given 150 years of atmospheric build-up of anthropogenic greenhouse gases.

Natural variability – important

> There is an increasing realisation that natural circulation patterns such as [El Niño-Southern Oscillation] and [North Atlantic Oscillation] play a fundamental role in global climate and its interannual and longer-term variability.
>
> IPCC, *Climate Change 2001: The Scientific Basis*, Cambridge University Press, Cambridge, 2001, p. 51

Rate of atmospheric GHG build-up – overmodelled

The 1 per cent/yr CO_2 increase represents the changes in radiative forcing due to all greenhouse gases, hence this is a higher rate than is projected for CO_2 alone. This increase of radiative forcing lies on the high side of the SRES scenarios [note also that CO_2 doubles around mid-21st century in most of the scenarios]. However, the experiments are valuable for promoting the understanding of differences in the model responses.

Ibid., p. 527

The rate of increase of atmospheric CO_2 concentration has been about 1.5 ppm (0.4 per cent) per year over the past two decades.

Ibid., p. 7

Satellite/balloon temperature records – modest warming

Over the shorter time period for which there have been both satellite and weather balloon data (since 1979), the balloon and satellite records show significantly less lower-troposphere warming than observed at the surface … The difference in the warming rates is statistically significant.

Ibid., pp. 27–28

Reduced temperature variation
(decreasing diurnal cycle)

On average, between 1950 and 1993, night-time daily minimum air temperatures over land increased by about 0.2°C per decade. This is about twice the rate of increase in daytime daily maximum air temperatures (0.1°C per decade.)

Ibid., p. 2

Since 1950 it is very likely that there has been a reduction in the frequency of extreme low temperatures with a smaller increase in the frequency of extreme high temperatures.

Ibid., p. 4

New analyses of daily maximum and minimum land-surface temperatures for 1950 to 1993 continue to show that this measure of diurnal temperature range is decreasing very widely, although not everywhere. On average, minimum temperatures are increasing at about twice the rate of maximum temperatures (0.2 versus 0.1°C/decade).

Ibid., p. 27

Changes in total cloud amounts over Northern Hemisphere mid and high latitude continental regions indicate a likely increase in cloud cover of about 2 per cent since the beginning of the 20th century, which has now been shown to be positively correlated with decreases in the diurnal temperature range.

Ibid., p. 30

Night minimum temperatures are continuing to increase, lengthening the freeze-free season in many mid and high latitude regions. There has been a reduction in the frequency of extreme low temperatures, without an equivalent increase in the frequency of extreme high temperatures.

Ibid., p. 101

A significant reduction in the frequency of extreme low monthly and seasonal average temperatures across much of the globe has occurred since the late 19th century. However, a relatively smaller increase in the frequency of extreme high monthly and seasonal average temperatures has been observed.

Ibid., p. 104

Since the 1950s both daily maximum and minimum temperatures are available over more than 50 per cent of the global land area. These data indicate that on average the mean minimum temperature has increased at nearly twice the rate of the maximum temperature, reducing the daily temperature range by about 0.8°C over these areas.

Ibid., p. 106

The overall global trend for the maximum temperature during 1950 to 1993 is approximately 0.1°C/decade and the trend for the minimum temperature is about 0.2°C/decade. Consequently, the trend in the [diurnal temperature range] is about –0.1°C/decade.

Ibid., p. 108

As reported in the [IPCC Second Assessment Report (1995)], and updated by Easterling et al. (1997), the increase in temperature in recent decades has involved a faster rise in daily minimum than daily maximum temperature in many continental regions. This gives a decrease in the diurnal temperature range (DTR) in many parts of the world.

Ibid., p. 108

New analyses of mean daily maximum and minimum temperatures continue to support a reduction in the diurnal temperature range with minimum temperatures increasing about twice the rate of maximum temperatures over the second half of the 20th century.

Ibid., p. 129

Sub-freezing warming concentration

Based on recent global model simulations, it is very likely that nearly all land areas will warm more rapidly than the global average, particularly those at northern high latitudes in the cold season.

Ibid., p. 13

In accord with the results in the [IPCC Second Assessment Report (1995)], recent warming (1976 to 2000) has been greatest over the mid-latitude Northern Hemisphere continents in winter ... Over 1901 to 2000 as a whole, noting the strong consistence across the land–ocean boundary, most warming is observed over mid and high latitude Asia and parts of western Canada.

Ibid., pp. 116–17

Sea level rise – falling estimates

Global mean sea level is projected to rise by 0.09 to 0.88 metres between 1990 and 2100, for the full range of [IPCC Special Report on Emission Scenarios] … The range of sea level rise presented in the SAR was 0.13 to 0.94 metres based on the IS92 scenarios. Despite the higher temperature change projections in this assessment, the sea level projections are slightly lower, primarily due to the use of improved models, which give a smaller contribution from glaciers and ice sheets.

Ibid., p. 16

Based on the very few long tide-gauge records, the average rate of sea level rise has been larger during the 20th century than during the 19th century. No significant acceleration in the rate of sea level rise during the 20th century has been detected. This is not inconsistent with model results due to the possibility of compensating factors and the limited data.

Ibid., p. 31

No significant acceleration in the rate of sea level rise during the 20th century has been detected. … There is decadal variability in extreme sea levels but no evidence of widespread increases in extremes other than that associated with a change in the mean.

Ibid., p. 641

The West Antarctic ice sheet has attracted special attention because it contains enough ice to raise sea level by 6m and because of suggestions that instabilities associated with it being grounded below sea level may result in rapid ice discharge when the surrounding ice shelves are weakened … It is now widely agreed that major loss of grounded ice and accelerated sea level rise are very unlikely during the 21st century.

Ibid., p. 642

Within present uncertainties, observations and models are both consistent with a lack of significant acceleration of sea level rise during the 20th century.

Ibid., p. 699

Weather extremes not increasing

No systematic changes in the frequency of tornadoes, thunder days, or hail events are evident in the limited areas analysed.

Ibid., p. 5

For some other extreme phenomena, many of which may have important impacts on the environment and society, there is currently insufficient information to assess recent trends, and climate models currently lack the spatial detail required to make confident projections. For example, very small-scale phenomena, such as thunderstorms, tornadoes, hail and lightning, are not simulated in climate models.

Ibid., p. 15

Current [climate model] projections show little change or a small increase in amplitude for El Niño events over the next 100 years.

Ibid., p. 16

There is no compelling evidence to indicate that the characteristics of tropical and extratropical storms have changed.

Ibid., p. 33

Based on limited data, the observed variations in the intensity and frequency of tropical and extra-tropical cyclones and severe local storms show no clear trends in the last half of the 20th century, although multi-decadal fluctuations are sometimes apparent.

Ibid., p. 34

Changes in tropical and extra-tropical storm intensity and frequency are dominated by inter-decadal to multi-decadal variations, with no significant trends over the 20th century evident. Conflicting analyses make it difficult to draw definitive conclusions about changes in storm activity, especially in the extra-tropics.

Ibid., p. 104

Surprises – very speculative

The possibility for rapid and irreversible changes in the climate system exists, but there is a large degree of uncertainty about the mechanisms involved and hence also about the likelihood or time-scales of such transitions.

Ibid., p. 53

Increased precipitation – not much

It is very likely that precipitation has increased by 0.5 to 1 per cent per decade in the 20th century over most mid and high latitudes of the Northern Hemisphere continents, and it is likely that rainfall has increased by 0.2 to 0.3 per cent per decade over the tropical (10°N to 10°S) land areas.

Ibid., p. 4

Over the 20th century (1900 to 1995), there were relatively small increases in global land areas experiencing severe drought or severe wetness.

Ibid., p. 33

Feedback effects – the key uncertainty

Within the boundary layer (roughly the lowest 1 to 2km of the atmosphere), water vapour increases with increasing temperature. In the free troposphere above the boundary layer, where the water vapour greenhouse effect is most important, the situation is harder to quantify. Water vapour feedback, as derived from current models, approximately doubles the warming from what it would be for fixed water vapour. Since the SAR (second assessment report), major improvements have occurred in the treatment of water vapour in models, although detrainment of moisture from clouds remains quite uncertain and discrepancies exist between model water vapour distributions and those observed.

Ibid., p. 49

As has been the case since the first IPCC Assessment Report in 1990, probably the greatest uncertainty in future projections of climate arises from clouds and their interactions with radiation. Clouds can both absorb and reflect solar radiation (thereby cooling the surface) and absorb and emit long wave radiation (thereby warming the surface).

Ibid., p. 49

In the free troposphere above the boundary layer, where the water vapour greenhouse effect is most important, the behaviour of water vapour cannot be inferred from simple thermodynamic arguments. Free tropospheric water vapour is governed by a variety of dynamical and microphysical influences which are represented with varying degrees of fidelity in general circulation models.

Ibid., p. 421

It has been estimated that, without changes in the relative area of convective and dry regions, a shift of water vapour to lower levels in the dry regions could, at the extreme, lead to a halving of the currently estimated water vapour feedback, but could not actually cause it to become a negative, stabilising feedback.

Ibid., p. 425

Since the SAR, appraisal of the confidence in simulated water vapour feedback has shifted from a diffuse concern about upper-tropospheric humidity to a more focused concern about the role of microphysical processes in the convection parametrizations, and particularly those affecting tropical deep convection. Further progress will almost certainly require abandoning the artificial diagnostic separation between water vapour and cloud feedbacks.

Ibid., p. 427

Climate modelling – tentative

[Climate] models cannot yet simulate all aspects of climate (e.g., they still cannot account fully for the observed trend in the surface-troposphere temperature difference since 1979), and there are particular uncertainties associated with clouds and their interaction with radiation and aerosols.

Ibid., p. 9

Clouds represent a significant source of potential error in climate simulations. The possibility that models underestimate systematically solar absorption in clouds remains a controversial matter. The sign of the net cloud feedback is still a matter of uncertainty, and the various models exhibit a large spread. Further uncertainties arise from precipitation processes and the difficulty in correctly simulating the diurnal cycle and precipitation amounts and frequencies.

Ibid., pp. 49–50

Some progress has been made in reducing uncertainty [in climate modelling], though ... the sources of uncertainty ... include discrepancies between the vertical profile of temperature change in the troposphere seen in observations and models ... large uncertainties in estimates of internal climate variability from models and observations ... considerable uncertainty in the reconstructions of solar and volcanic forcing which are based on proxy or limited observational data for all but the last two decades ... large uncertainties in anthropogenic forcing ... associated with the effects of aerosols ... [and] large differences in the response of different models to the same forcing.

Ibid., pp. 59–61

Aerosol cooling – in dispute

The radiative forcing due to aerosols depends not only on
... special distributions, but also on the size, shape, and
chemical of the particles and various aspects (e.g. cloud
formation) of the hydrological cycle as well. As a result of all
of these factors, obtaining accurate estimates of this forcing
has been very challenging, from both the observational and
theoretical standpoints.

Ibid., p. 44

The effect of the increasing amount of aerosols on the
radiative forcing is complex and not yet well known.

Ibid., p. 93

Regional forecasting – not reliable

To date, a relatively high level of uncertainty has
characterised regional climate change information. This
is due to the complexity of the processes that determine
regional climate change, which span a wide range of spatial
and temporal scales, and to the difficulty in extracting fine-
scale regional information from coarse resolution coupled
Atmosphere-Ocean General Circulation Models (AOGCMs).

Ibid., p. 587

The difficulty of simulating regional climate change
is ... evident. The effects of forcings and circulations
at the planetary, regional and local scale need to be
properly represented, along with the teleconnection
effects of regional forcing anomalies. These processes are
characterised by a range of temporal variability scales, and
can be highly non-linear. In addition, similarly to what

happens for the global Earth system, regional climate is also modulated by interactions among different components of the climate system, such as the atmosphere, hydrosphere, cryosphere, biosphere and chemosphere, which may require coupling of these components at the regional scale.

Ibid., p. 588

Despite recent improvements and developments, regionalisation research is still a maturing process and the related uncertainties are still rather poorly known ... Therefore a coherent picture of regional climate change via available regionalisation techniques cannot yet be drawn.

Ibid., p. 623

APPENDIX C   W. S. JEVONS – FIRST CRITIC OF RENEWABLE ENERGY

William Stanley Jevons (1835–82) founded natural resource economics with his 1865 book *The Coal Question: An Inquiry Concerning the Progress of the Nation, and the Probable Exhaustion of Our Coal Mines*. Jevons, who applied the gloomy theory of Thomas Robert Malthus (1766–1834) to energy, warned that coal depletion in England would increase energy costs and threaten Britain's future as an economic power.

Jevons failed to envisage the rise of petroleum and natural gas as primary energies in the world market. He also failed to comprehend how the supply of coal in his home country, as elsewhere, could expand from growing financial resources and new applications of the 'master resource', *human ingenuity*.

What Jevons *did* understand and correctly envisaged in his early day was the inability of renewable energies to re-emerge as primary energies after the coal age (really the carbon energy age). The challenges posed by renewables' intermittency/variability, land/siting constraints and low energy concentration have remained to this day. A fourth problem was not seen by Jevons given his Malthusian worldview – the competitive challenge for renewable technologies given their very high up-front capital costs competing against lower-cost technologies fuelled by carbon energies with flat-to-declining prices.

These quotations from the first edition of *The Coal Question* make points that still have applicability. Compare Jevons's conclusions with a summary of the renewable energy problem made 137 years later in a feature article in *Science*:

> All renewables suffer from low areal power densities. ...
> Renewables are intermittent dispersed sources unsuited
> to baseload without transmission, storage, and power
> conditioning. Wind power is often available only from
> remote or offshore locations. Meeting local demand with
> [photovoltaic] arrays today requires pumped-storage or
> battery-electric backup systems of comparable or greater
> capacity.[1]

Wind power

> The first great requisite of motive power is, *that it shall be
> wholly at our command, to be exerted when, and where, and
> in what degree we desire*. The wind, for instance, as a direct
> motive power, is wholly inapplicable to a system of machine
> labour, for during a calm season the whole business of the
> country would be thrown out of gear.
>
> > William Stanley Jevons, *The Coal Question: An Inquiry Concerning the
> > Progress of the Nation, and the Probable Exhaustion of our Coal Mines*,
> > Macmillan, London, 1865, p. 122

> No possible concentration of windmills ... would supply the
> force required in large factories or iron works. An ordinary
> windmill has the power of about thirty-four men, or at most
> seven horses. Many ordinary factories would therefore
> require ten windmills to drive them, and the great Dowlais

---

1   Hoffert et al., op. cit., p. 984.

Ironworks, employing a total engine power of 7,308 horses, would require no less than 1,000 large windmills!

Ibid., p. 123

Before the era of steam-engines, windmills were tried for draining mines, 'but, though they were powerful machines, they were very irregular, so that in a long tract of calm weather the mines were drowned, and all the workmen thrown idle. From this cause, the contingent expenses of these machines were very great; besides, they were only applicable in open and elevated situations.'

Ibid., p. 123

Richard Lovell Edgeworth spent forty years' labour in trying to bring wind carriages into use. But no ingenuity could prevent [wind carriages] from being uncertain; and their rapidity with a strong breeze was such, that … 'they seemed to fly, rather than roll along the ground.' Such rapidity not under full control must be in the highest degree dangerous.

Ibid., p. 126

A wind-wagon would undoubtedly be the cheapest kind of conveyance if it would always go the right way. Simon Stevin invented such a carriage, which carried twenty-eight persons, and is said to have gone seven leagues an hour.

Ibid., p. 125

Hydropower

When an abundant natural fall of water is at hand, nothing can be cheaper or better than water power. But everything depends upon local circumstances. The occasional mountain torrent is simply destructive. Many streams and rivers only contain sufficient water half the year round and costly reservoirs alone could keep up the summer supply. In flat countries no engineering art could procure any considerable supply of natural water power, and in very few places do we find water power free from occasional failure by drought.

Ibid., p. 129

The necessity … of carrying the work to the power, not the power to the work, is a disadvantage in water power, and wholly prevents that concentration of works in one neighbourhood which is highly advantageous to the perfection of our mechanical system. Even the cost of conveying materials often overbalances the cheapness of water power.

Ibid., p. 129

Biomass

We cannot revert to timber fuel, for 'nearly the entire surface of our island would be required to grow timber sufficient for the consumption of the iron manufacture alone.'

Ibid., p. 140

Geothermal

The internal heat of the earth … presents an immense store of force, but, being manifested only in the hot-spring, the volcano, or the warm mine, it is evidently not available.

Ibid., p. 120

ABOUT THE IEA

The Institute is a research and educational charity (No. CC 235 351), limited by guarantee. Its mission is to improve understanding of the fundamental institutions of a free society with particular reference to the role of markets in solving economic and social problems.

The IEA achieves its mission by:

- a high-quality publishing programme
- conferences, seminars, lectures and other events
- outreach to school and college students
- brokering media introductions and appearances

The IEA, which was established in 1955 by the late Sir Antony Fisher, is an educational charity, not a political organisation. It is independent of any political party or group and does not carry on activities intended to affect support for any political party or candidate in any election or referendum, or at any other time. It is financed by sales of publications, conference fees and voluntary donations.

In addition to its main series of publications the IEA also publishes a quarterly journal, *Economic Affairs*, and has two specialist programmes – Environment and Technology, and Education.

The IEA is aided in its work by a distinguished international Academic Advisory Council and an eminent panel of Honorary Fellows. Together with other academics, they review prospective IEA publications, their comments being passed on anonymously to authors. All IEA papers are therefore subject to the same rigorous independent refereeing process as used by leading academic journals.

IEA publications enjoy widespread classroom use and course adoptions in schools and universities. They are also sold throughout the world and often translated/reprinted.

Since 1974 the IEA has helped to create a world-wide network of 100 similar institutions in over 70 countries. They are all independent but share the IEA's mission.

Views expressed in the IEA's publications are those of the authors, not those of the Institute (which has no corporate view), its Managing Trustees, Academic Advisory Council members or senior staff.

Members of the Institute's Academic Advisory Council, Honorary Fellows, Trustees and Staff are listed on the following page.

The Institute gratefully acknowledges financial support for its publications programme and other work from a generous benefaction by the late Alec and Beryl Warren.

Other papers recently published by the IEA include:

WHO, What and Why?

Transnational Government, Legitimacy and the World Health Organization
Roger Scruton
Occasional Paper 113; ISBN 0 255 36487 3
£8.00

The World Turned Rightside Up

A New Trading Agenda for the Age of Globalisation
John C. Hulsman
Occasional Paper 114; ISBN 0 255 36495 4
£8.00

The Representation of Business in English Literature

Introduced and edited by Arthur Pollard
Readings 53; ISBN 0 255 36491 1
£12.00

Anti-Liberalism 2000

The Rise of New Millennium Collectivism
David Henderson
Occasional Paper 115; ISBN 0 255 36497 0
£7.50

Capitalism, Morality and Markets

Brian Griffiths, Robert A. Sirico, Norman Barry & Frank Field
Readings 54; ISBN 0 255 36496 2
£7.50

A Conversation with Harris and Seldon

Ralph Harris & Arthur Seldon
Occasional Paper 116; ISBN 0 255 36498 9
£7.50

Malaria and the DDT Story

Richard Tren & Roger Bate
Occasional Paper 117; ISBN 0 255 36499 7
£10.00

A Plea to Economists Who Favour Liberty: Assist the Everyman

Daniel B. Klein
Occasional Paper 118; ISBN 0 255 36501 2
£10.00

Waging the War of Ideas

John Blundell
Occasional Paper 119; ISBN 0 255 36500 4
£10.00

The Changing Fortunes of Economic Liberalism

Yesterday, Today and Tomorrow
David Henderson
Occasional Paper 105 (new edition); ISBN 0 255 36520 9
£12.50

The Global Education Industry

Lessons from Private Education in Developing Countries
James Tooley
Hobart Paper 141 (new edition); ISBN 0 255 36503 9
£12.50

Saving Our Streams

The Role of the Anglers' Conservation Association in
Protecting English and Welsh Rivers
Roger Bate
Research Monograph 53; ISBN 0 255 36494 6
£10.00

Better Off Out?

The Benefits or Costs of EU Membership
Brian Hindley & Martin Howe
Occasional Paper 99 (new edition); ISBN 0 255 36502 0
£10.00

Buckingham at 25

Freeing the Universities from State Control
Edited by James Tooley
Readings 55; ISBN 0 255 36512 8
£15.00

Lectures on Regulatory and Competition Policy

Irwin M. Stelzer
Occasional Paper 120; ISBN 0 255 36511 X
£12.50

Misguided Virtue

False Notions of Corporate Social Responsibility
David Henderson
Hobart Paper 142; ISBN 0 255 36510 1
£12.50

HIV and Aids in Schools

The Political Economy of Pressure Groups and Miseducation
Barrie Craven, Pauline Dixon, Gordon Stewart & James Tooley
Occasional Paper 121; ISBN 0 255 36522 5
£10.00

The Road to Serfdom
The Reader's Digest *condensed version*
Friedrich A. Hayek
Occasional Paper 122; ISBN 0 255 36530 6
£7.50

Bastiat's *The Law*
Introduction by Norman Barry
Occasional Paper 123; ISBN 0 255 36509 8
£7.50

A Globalist Manifesto for Public Policy
Charles Calomiris
Occasional Paper 124; ISBN 0 255 36525 X
£7.50

Euthanasia for Death Duties
Putting Inheritance Tax Out of Its Misery
Barry Bracewell-Milnes
Research Monograph 54; ISBN 0 255 36513 6
£10.00

Liberating the Land

The Case for Private Land-use Planning

Mark Pennington

Hobart Paper 143; ISBN 0 255 36508 X

£10.00

IEA Yearbook of Government Performance 2002/2003

Edited by Peter Warburton

Yearbook 1; ISBN 0 255 36532 2

£15.00

Britain's Relative Economic Performance, 1870–1999

Nicholas Crafts

Research Monograph 55; ISBN 0 255 36524 1

£10.00

Should We Have Faith in Central Banks?

Otmar Issing

Occasional Paper 125; ISBN 0 255 36528 4

£7.50

The Dilemma of Democracy

Arthur Seldon

Hobart Paper 136 (reissue); ISBN 0 255 36536 5

£10.00

Capital Controls: a 'Cure' Worse Than the Problem?

Forrest Capie

Research Monograph 56; ISBN 0 255 36506 3

£10.00

The Poverty of 'Development Economics'

Deepak Lal

Hobart Paper 144 (reissue); ISBN 0 255 36519 5

£15.00

Should Britain Join the Euro?

The Chancellor's Five Tests Examined

Patrick Minford

Occasional Paper 126; ISBN 0 255 36527 6

£7.50

Post-Communist Transition: Some Lessons

Leszek Balcerowicz

Occasional Paper 127; ISBN 0 255 36533 0

£7.50

A Tribute to Peter Bauer

John Blundell et al.

Occasional Paper 128; ISBN 0 255 36531 4

£10.00

Employment Tribunals

Their Growth and the Case for Radical Reform

J. R. Shackleton

Hobart Paper 145; ISBN 0 255 36515 2

£10.00

Fifty Economic Fallacies Exposed

Geoffrey E. Wood

Occasional Paper 129; ISBN 0 255 36518 7

£12.50

A Market in Airport Slots

Keith Boyfield (editor), David Starkie, Tom Bass & Barry Humphreys

Readings 56; ISBN 0 255 36505 5

£10.00

Money, Inflation and the Constitutional Position of the Central Bank

Milton Friedman & Charles A. E. Goodhart

Readings 57; ISBN 0 255 36538 1

£10.00

Railway.com
Parallels between the early British railways and the ICT revolution
Robert C. B. Miller
Research Monograph 57; ISBN 0 255 36534 9
£12.50

The Regulation of Financial Markets
Edited by Philip Booth & David Currie
Readings 58; ISBN 0 255 36551 9
£12.50

To order copies of currently available IEA papers, or to enquire about availability, please contact:

Lavis Marketing
IEA orders
FREEPOST LON21280
Oxford OX3 7BR

Tel: 01865 767575
Fax: 01865 750079
Email: orders@lavismarketing.co.uk

The IEA also offers a subscription service to its publications. For a single annual payment, currently £40.00 in the UK, you will receive every title the IEA publishes across the course of a year, invitations to events, and discounts on our extensive back catalogue. For more information, please contact:

Subscriptions
The Institute of Economic Affairs
2 Lord North Street
London SW1P 3LB

Tel: 020 7799 8900
Fax: 020 7799 2137
Website: www.iea.org.uk